Liberal Education

By MARK VAN DOREN

With a new Preface by the author

Beacon Press   *Beacon Hill*   Boston

To

WILLIAM SLOANE

LC
1011
V3
1959

Contents

Mark Van Doren, one of America's most distinguished men of letters, was born at Hope, Illinois, in 1894. He received an A.B. from the University of Illinois in 1914, an A.M. from the same university in 1915, a Ph.D. from Columbia University in 1920, and several honorary degrees in recent years, including a Litt.D. from the University of Illinois in 1958. A long-standing member of the Columbia University faculty, where he has been Professor of English since 1942, he has been guest lecturer at St. John's College in Maryland, literary editor and motion picture critic for *The Nation,* and participant in the radio programs "Invitation to Learning" and "The Eternal Light." He lives with his wife, Dorothy Graffe Van Doren, in Falls Village, Connecticut.

A writer of many facets, his COLLECTED POEMS received the Pulitzer prize in 1940. He published a play, THE LAST DAYS OF LINCOLN, in 1959. He has written novels, short stories, and numerous books in the field of literary criticism, including HENRY DAVID THOREAU, THE POETRY OF JOHN DRYDEN, SHAKESPEARE, THE NOBLE VOICE, NATHANIEL HAWTHORNE, INTRODUCTION TO POETRY, and DON QUIXOTE'S PROFESSION, and is the editor of several anthologies, the best known of which is AN ANTHOLOGY OF WORLD POETRY. In 1958 he published THE AUTOBIOGRAPHY OF MARK VAN DOREN.

PREFACE TO THE BEACON PRESS EDITION

The original occasion of this book was a world war. Appearing in the middle year of that war, 1943, it addressed itself to the question whether liberal education would survive its suspension during a time when everything else thought to be a luxury had likewise been suspended. And yet that was not quite my question either, for I knew that liberal education would return. It was rather this: how good would it be, and at the very best how good *could* it be, when it came back? My interest was in the timeless thing that never changes its essential form, the thing that cannot be thought about well in moods of panic or desperate haste. "The need," I said, was for "a definition of liberal education whenever and however it manages to exist." In the preface to a later edition of 1948 I remarked that "the problems of education do not change, so that the ensuing text retains whatever validity it once had." I removed certain references to a no longer contemporary war, and of course in the present edition they are not restored. But neither in the text itself is there any recognition of another crisis now said to be upon us, born of cold war, global rivalries, and the sensational pre-eminence of science and technology in public talk.

It is not that I consider the crisis unreal. It is so real, surely, that the best possible thinking should be done about it. And since liberal education is intellectual education, its relevance might seem never to have been greater. And so it never was. But what is the relevance of liberal education at any time? Why is it always a necessity, not a luxury? And how should it behave in crises? I still believe that it should behave like itself; there is no other way in which it can be useful. So I let my definition of it stand, for whatever it may continue to be worth.

Science is not the only problem, yet it is a huge one, and it always was. There has never been a time in Western thought when science was not a problem. So it was natural enough for me to say in 1943 that the task of liberal education was the task "of knowing what to do about science. But that will mean," I added, "knowing science as even science does not know itself today." Science, my amateur's observation of it still moves me to remark, is strangely nervous about itself. Scientists doubt their own wisdom; they are afraid they will kill the very race they are supposed to serve. The layman is curiously divided between a conviction that only science will save us and a fear that it will make life impossible. He thinks he is not wise, and now he wonders if any scientist is, or could be even in the best conditions. This is the age of science: an age, oddly enough, in which it might be said that we know less than ever before what we are doing. Clearly there is a great deal to be thought about these days. And the conviction underlying this book is that as many persons as possible should do the thinking. Too few now recognize their responsibility. The age of science is an age of experts. It is also, judging by what most people say about themselves, an age of ignorance.

It would be less so if liberal education were more perfect. Liberal education can never be quite perfect, since it is ideal; but at any given time it is good in proportion to the clarity with which it is conceived and the effort which that clarity inspires. One unmistakable sign that it is good is that opinion flourishes and argument goes on: argument, that is to say, about the greatest things, the difficult, the all but insoluble things that haunt us every morning as we wake. An unmistakable sign of its lapse would be a general disposition to leave things to those who are understood as specializing in them. The best time for a free society is the time when everybody believes it makes a difference what he thinks and knows; and the accent should be at last on *knows*. The only insurance against disaster is knowledge, widely diffused.

An all too common synonym for "liberal" is "broad" or "general." Breadth and generality are fine things, but we should not be vague in our understanding of them. When we are precise in our understanding of them we mean that we assume a power in them to help us judge particulars: to ask specific questions and demand specific answers. The broadest mind knows the greatest number of things: related things, of course, but still they are things. The mind has been there, and has been at work. Nor when its opinion is desired does it retreat into attitudes and views. When we go to a wise man for advice it is not to learn what he knows about everything; it is to benefit by what he knows about the single thing that troubles us. If he seems to bring vast considerations to bear upon it, well and good; we should scarcely be comfortable otherwise; but what we want in the end is his opinion as to here, to now, to this. The surest proof that any mind is free is its faith in itself when faced with hard questions. It may not be sure that it can solve them, but it does not doubt its capacity to make the attempt.

Knowledge is both applauded and despised. Less often is it recognized as what it surely is: the end product of all human effort. It was the one thing that Socrates desired; and when Dante called Aristotle "master" he said what he meant by the word: "master of those that know." Men hunger for knowledge now as much as they ever did. They would like to *know* whether the welfare state is in the long run to be good or bad for them; whether outer space is worth travelling in; whether peace is possible, and by what means. But sometimes it appears that they do not expect their hunger to be satisfied, at least by any means at their personal disposal. And too many of them are content with the prospect of starvation. There is no knowledge in such fields, they say; or if there is, only calamity will expose it.

Liberal education does not claim to provide this kind of knowledge by itself. The most it claims is that it prepares the intellect to search for it and to recognize it when or if it is available. The process of preparation, however, involves knowledge too: of the intellect, and of its powers. Liberal education is concerned with these. And if its status is no higher than it was in 1943, the reason could be that the intellect is not valued in our society as the simple thing it is: an instrument whereby the truth may be discovered. Those who scorn it, or who doubt its reality, in all likelihood assume a grander function: fancy or fraudulent as the case might be, but grander certainly. Whereas it is as lowly — as deadly, too — as the sentences of Socrates. It is a precision instrument, no more fancy than a surgeon's knife.

The process of preparation involves knowledge of the mind's precision, and practice in the use of it; but still another knowledge must be there. This is the knowledge of how men before our time have used their minds: scientists, philosophers, historians, geometers, and poets. The student who undergoes a liberal education is claiming an inheritance without which he would be lost in the world he inhabits. And one precious thing about this inheritance is that it acquaints him with precision in more than one field where he is likely to think it operates today. That is the field of science, where everyone knows it operates. And if the student doubts that it operates anywhere else, there are those who share the doubt. But the precision of Shakespeare was marvelous too: and of Mozart; and of Dante; and of Plato. Liberal education, by introducing him to precision on many fronts, can make him at home with the intellect at its happiest, even though most of its masters are dead. To him they will not be dead; and to that extent his own life increases, for he knows how to think of every great mind as his contemporary. He is prepared then to add to the whole glory if he can.

But he is only prepared. The fruits of a liberal education are still to come. Yet they will not come unless the preparation is precise. Liberal education, I said in 1943, "is a specific discipline, and I have tried to show that it has rules; also an inescapable content." I am not aware that during the years since then there has been much agreement with this claim. The claim, incidentally, was not for my own views of the discipline in question; it was rather for the proposition that the discipline exists, if only ideally, and for the further proposition that the chief duty of teachers is to discover its content. Any college can be better than it is; but all colleges would be better if those in charge of them considered together, at regular intervals, the ideal college curriculum. They would not need to fear that every college would then become identical with every other; such identities cannot exist in nature. But if all liberal colleges had the same aim, and if they were serious in their pursuit of it, the differences among them would become, for a change, really interesting.

This is something like the question of the individual student, whoever and wherever he is. The notion persists that he is the chief concern of education. In one sense he certainly is: we want all the individuals we can get, and we want the best ones possible. But it remains a real question how we get them; I suspect it is not by trimming education to what is supposed to be their individual needs. I continue to believe that the way to produce individual intellects is to teach all students the same things, and of course the best things. They will make their own responses, and discover their own ideas; but these will be best when the material for study has been the kind of material that is good for everybody. Members of any modern society need to know a great many things in common. How they know them may be an individual matter, but whether they know them can make a fatal difference. The future of the world may depend upon how many do. And the question that presses, if any question does, is what shall everybody know?

The question reaches as deep as the elementary and the secondary school, where illiteracy, whether in mathematics or in language and literature, presumably can be prevented. It is increasingly apparent that either kind of illiteracy will in time endanger all mankind. The most insistent question is one of standards; and after that, of how uniform they should be throughout the country. It is a question not to be dismissed lightly. It might very well be one of the great questions which liberal education is not equipped to answer. Yet it could be a preparation for the answer, provided it be true to its own self.

MARK VAN DOREN

I

Nobody Thinks He Is Educated

Tʜɪs is a happy land, proud of everything it possesses, including innumerable schools, colleges, and universities where droves of young persons beam with a perpetual morning smile. Education is almost unnecessary for a people that knows and loves its destiny so well.

This is a worried generation, doubting the quality of its life and indulging in attacks upon itself for which history provides no parallel until we reach the Major Prophets. It is an insecure age, dubious of its foundations and full of rumors that they are shaken daily. Aberrations once dismissed as normal to mankind are suddenly terrible, and must be corrected or suppressed. We have lost the art of laughing at such things. We call them tragic dislocations, deep-seated signs of an ill time. Our appetite for life is gone with a relish for the game of noting and naming imperfections. We are far from assuming that education is superfluous. So far, in fact, that nobody is to be found who considers himself educated at all.

Which legend is true? Both are, but the latter one states itself more loudly. It is impossible to discover a man who believes that the right things were done to his mind. He was forced to learn too many things, or too few. It was all too general; or too special. The present was ignored; or the past. Something was left out entirely, or at best skimmed over: mathematics, poetry, the method of science, the secret of religion, the history of this or that. The result is, he will say, that he does not feel at home in the realms of nature and intellect; he is not securely centered between thoughts and things; he is not a philosopher. And whereas once he did not care, now—if he is middle-aged—he does. He knows he has missed something, and he suspects that all the king's horses could not find it for him again.

As for the education of others, a constant chorus of voices reminds him that no such thing exists. Or that if it does it is pernicious. One journalist asserts that "the prevailing education is destined, if it continues, to destroy Western civilization, and is in fact destroying it." Another one says in despair: "As far as I know, there does not exist a university or an undergraduate college, in the traditional and proper sense, anywhere in the country." And not too long ago the president of a famous university published his conviction that "today, though it is possible to get an education in an American university, a man would have to be so bright and know so much to get it that he wouldn't really need it."

Perhaps no age has thought its education good enough. Life itself is never good enough; and the job of education, which is to remedy the defect, doubtless cannot be done. If life were perfect there would be no need of education; there is none in Utopia. But life remains imperfect, and so does education.

Twenty-four centuries ago, in Athens itself, the mother

city of our mind, Aristotle could record a prevailing uncertainty as to what education ought to be. "There are doubts concerning the business of it," he wrote, "since all people do not agree in those things they would have a child taught, both with respect to improvement in virtue and a happy life; nor is it clear whether the object of it should be to improve the reason or rectify the morals. From the present mode of education we cannot determine with certainty to which men incline, whether to instruct a child in what will be useful to him in life, or what tends to virtue, or what is excellent; for all these things have their separate defenders." The issues we find ourselves so impotent to settle—and impotence makes men angry—are as ancient as that, though we have other names for them now. They are the issues between moral and intellectual education, and between liberal and technical training. More will be heard about them as this book proceeds.

The uneasiness, then, may be eternal. Less than one century ago it was felt with equal force in America, by Emerson. "It is ominous," he said, "that this word Education has so cold, so hopeless a sound. A treatise on education, a convention on education, affects us with slight paralysis and a certain yawning of the jaws. Our culture has truckled to the times. It is not manworthy. If the vast and the spiritual are omitted, so are the practical and the moral. It does not make us brave or free. We teach boys to be such men as we are. We do not teach them to aspire to be all they can. We do not give them a training as if we believed in their noble nature. We scarce educate their bodies. We do not train the eye and the hand. We exercise their understandings to the apprehension and comparison of some facts, to a skill in numbers, in words; we aim to make accountants, attorneys, engineers; but not to make able, earnest, great-hearted men." Such sentences, allowing for the fact that most of us today are afraid to be as moral as that, have a familiar ring. Education has never been right.

Yet the uneasiness has seldom been as acute as it is now; and for the particular reason that the times to which our culture truckles, if that is the fair word for it, are themselves so desperate and demanding. Education is being asked on every hand to save the world; not merely to "run a race with the spirit of the age," as William Whewell once put it, but to see to it that the age survives at all, whether in spirit or in body. Now these virtues and now those are ordered to be taught, now this information and now that. One decade fears that peace is neglected; another, war. We hear about a race between violence and understanding, between ideas and machines. Civilization, now as at other times, must be wary of its outward enemies, but the true enemy is within us and will eat on there until our hollowness of heart and head can by some miracle be cured. Not a day passes but education is told that it fights from the last ditch.

And in a sense it does. The world is in such a sore state that education would be its nurse if it could. It too knows pity; it is by ancient tradition one of the healing arts. Yet it can be pardoned for responding with bewilderment to the demand that it medicine at once a sick society. Its supreme artist, Socrates, called himself a midwife; but he ministered to one man at a time. Education still does not know how it can lift a world at least as heavy as itself— at least indeed, for of course the world outweighs it. Education is a part of life, and the part does not direct the whole.

NOBODY THINKS HE IS EDUCATED

It has long been noted that a circular relation exists between education and society. Each depends upon the other to improve it; neither knows whether it is the acorn or the oak. One assumption, however, it has been customary for society to make concerning education: it has its own business to remember, and had better be left free to do it. The mass of men still suppose, naïvely and correctly, that learning keeps a certain distance from life; that universities are places where permanent things are known and the past remains available; that in crises the people should go to the professors, not the professors come to the people. The gravest danger to education now is its own readiness to risk its dignity in a rush to keep up with events, to serve mankind in a low way which will sacrifice respect. The world needs it badly; but so badly that it must study to preserve itself so that it may again be needed, and possessed. It can easily prove so useful as to earn contempt. So while it broods upon its own improvement, as it always does, education can afford to ponder programs of being no less deeply than schedules of doing.

All educators are well-intentioned, but few of them reflect upon their intentions. Hundreds of them at this moment are breathlessly confessing that the past generation of students was not taught to believe enough things. There is little evidence, however, of a search into the metaphysics or even the psychology of belief; and there is less evidence of an anxiety in educators to believe something themselves. Belief has its place in the natural history of a mind. But what place? And how important is it? And how can it be called so that it comes? These are embarrassing questions, easier to postpone than to answer.

Meanwhile we witness more of that process in education

known as "tinkering." In the absence of a theory that would tell us what to do, we rearrange and polish the machinery of a system that by and large keeps running, or seems to keep running, under its inherited power. There are "plans" galore, but for instruction rather than education; the student is to learn "about" this instead of that, while learning itself languishes. For all our surface briskness in reform, we do not relinquish the pleasures of routine. The hardest thing in education is to be profound and simple; to find a theory; to keep the ends of education distant, and its practice difficult.

The layman, again naïvely and correctly, understands this very well. What confuses him now is our combination of complexity when we talk of methods and superficiality when we promise results. The wheels that will whisk his son through college are more numerous than he can count; but he is not told to expect the transformation inside the son which tradition takes to be the main thing. The educator would do well to consult this layman, and in his conversation with him to avoid language which can "only be understood," as Renan once remarked, "by a committee." After that he might consult the greatest scientists, philosophers, poets, historians, and technicians who happen to be alive. They would often agree with the layman in their notions of the main thing. Too often the educator is neither lay nor learned, but a bored fellow who mixes prescriptions wherein all the tastes are flat or bad. So much knowledge "about" one thing or another, and never the tincture of wisdom.

He might be reminded, too, by such discourse that much of the burden in education is safely left where it belongs, on the back of the student. Faculties are asked what they can do for boys and girls who come to them to "get" an education, and they have fallen into the habit of enumerating the things they will "give," as if a list were all. When education goes wrong, the subject of it is partly to blame. This is not said often enough or firmly enough for the young to heed it. They can benefit by knowing that education is something they must labor to give themselves. At best it is a mysterious process, the precise stages of which no one has named or numbered. A child's learning to talk and read remains miraculous; and so does the boy's growth to be an intellectual man. Teaching helps, and it should be as good as possible. But there is also the person to be taught, and he should have the desire no less than the ability. The world ahead of us in America suggests that we should expect about twice as much from our young men and women as we have been content in the relatively easy, lazy days of isolation to expect either from them or from ourselves. If this is true, no conceivable list of goods over the counter will be long enough. Education is up to them as it was up to Socrates, Milton, Locke, and Lincoln.

The good educator is very serious but also very sensible. And somewhere in his soul there is a saving lightness. He understands, to begin with, the meaning of a recent remark: "Not everything can be learned." Some things are never taught; they are simply known. Other things cannot in the nature of things be known, either by student or by teacher. And then there is that endless series of knowable things only a few of which can be bestowed upon the student during the fragment of his life he spends at school.

To be thus modest about the possibilities of education is not to put its importance down. It becomes truly important when its limits are seen. What cannot be done will not be attempted at the cost of discrediting the whole enterprise; but what can be done—and the doing of this makes all the difference—will be done as artists do things, with skill and thorough care, and with a reverence not hostile to high spirits.

As little attention as possible will be wasted on details of knowledge which the student is certain to forget. Such of them as point a principle need to be mastered; but then if a right relation is maintained between detail and principle, the detail will not be forgotten. It will become an item in the mind around which other details organize themselves as long as life lasts. It will be the means by which a man remembers his principles; which are not things of rote, but live in the region where we can see and touch them. The principles are the things to remember, but this is how they are remembered.

The good educator knows, too, that the secret of the discipline he imparts is not the final secret of existence. The world is not to become perfect, even with the best education for everybody. Education does not pose as insurance against error and sin. There will continue to be plenty of both in a universe which man did not create, and which he inhabits as a more or less refractory citizen. If war is a gigantic error, education alone cannot cure it, nor will it promise to do so if it knows its own good. It might as well promise to find every man the right wife, or guarantee that each of his children will be helpful to him in his old age. The comparison is not as trivial as it sounds. As every man must manage these things as well as he may, so the world of men must manage itself. With education it can be wiser, but deeper things decide its fate.

Modesty in an educator bases itself, furthermore, upon

his perception that accident plays a high role in the affairs of human life, including the affair of education. No system can provide all the proper accidents for every person. If they were proper they would not be accidents. We do not arrange to meet those individuals who will become our friends; out of the billion women on earth only a few present themselves to the choice of a man who would be married; one does not decide what country to be born in, what hemisphere, what sex; one is, in short, less one's own destiny than it is agreeable to suppose. So in education the identity of a given teacher, the chance that one thing rather than another shall be heard, seen, or done at the precise moment when it will be most meaningful, and the further chance that attention will be adequate when a golden word is uttered—these matters, and many others, are matters of accident which the honest educator will not pretend he has the omniscience to order. He too is but a man.

That is what we want him to be, rather than a little god or a big machine. As a man he will know that his task is mysterious enough to make him modest; but he will also command the courage to see it in the simplest outline available to understanding. And he will mean by education his own as well as that of others. His own will not wither while he works, for what he works at is incidentally the best education for himself: one which perhaps he wishes he had had when he was younger, but which in any event he is pursuing now. Everett Dean Martin has warned the world against those who would educate it for anything less than the common intellectual good; who would impose disciplines with condescension, or in the cynicism of a taste for authority. Education is humble at the center; "one must come to it with clean hands and a pure heart or one can never know the secret power of it." This is true no less for the student than for the teacher. Clean hands in the learner's case mean a desire to know those things which are most worth knowing, not for his advantage but in themselves; and they mean a willingness to work for them as something not casually got or mechanically given.

The courage in the educator that makes him labor at the outline of his task will push him on, virtue being with him, to take the risk of action; he will not only see an outline, he will form his institution in harmony with the vision. This may involve mistakes, but he would rather make mistakes than linger in confusion. "Next to being right in the world," says Thomas Henry Huxley, "the best of all things is to be clearly and definitely wrong, because you will come out somewhere. If you go buzzing about between right and wrong, vibrating and fluctuating, you come out nowhere; but if you are absolutely and thoroughly and persistently wrong, you must, some of these days, have the extreme good fortune of knocking your head against a fact, and that sets you all straight again." Fact in the present instance may mean a better theory from elsewhere; or it may mean a sudden discovery that the students are unhappy; or it may mean that the outline fades because the educator's eyesight has improved. Whatever has happened, there is now a new step to take, but the feet of the explorer are firm.

When educators do not labor at the outline, others who are their subordinates, whether students or teachers, will. The one intolerable thing in education is the absence of intellectual design. American colleges today are not without their younger members who meet occasionally in an odd room to consider design. Their elders are busy handling the machine they inherited; these are concerned with discovering whether it has a heart. Most of the time it has not; but it will, for unless education is to die they are bound to have their way. Nothing so big can long remain meaningless. Education with an intellectual design is liberal education— of which more hereafter. And much is made at the moment of the need to defend it. But young people know, even if the old do not, that the first need is to reform it. Like democracy, it can be saved only by being increased. We keep as much as we have by getting more.

Nobody today thinks he has enough of it—is willing, that is, to call himself educated. Humility aside, he means that he does not find in himself a reasonably deep and clear feeling about the bearings upon one another, and upon his own mind, of three things, to name no more: art, science, and religion. He has never been at the center from which these radiate—if there is a center. He would like to know that first of all, and to realize what knowledge of it means. His education so far has been one-sided: mostly mathematical, mostly literary, or mostly something else. My own has been radically so, and I confess it here. It has been what passes for a literary education—not, that is, an education equipping me to read Newton. I think I can read Shakespeare, and that is an important capacity to have; but I am not sure I do it well if I cannot read certain other men at all. Shakespeare's book is one of the greatest, but it has its peers, and some of them are Greek to me. Perhaps he was talking to his peers.

I say this to make it clear at the start that my book is not by one who considers himself educated. It is by one who still wishes to be, and who has set out to discover if he can of what the experience would consist. It is not to be, therefore, a book about literary education—which many persons,

I find, identify with liberal education. A liberal education is nothing less than a complete one: complete, the reader will understand, within the limits of human reason and imagination. Much is heard these days about the difficulty of knowing all there is to be known. It was always difficult to do so. But the generations have varied in their interpretation of the task, and none has been as sure as this one that the task is impossible. Impossible on what grounds? That is a question we do not ask carefully enough. Impossible with what result? That is a question we have only begun to ask, in terror born of wars not merely between nations but between mutually destructive refinements of skill and special knowledge. The original result, however, was confusion. It was the existence of many persons who wished they were educated and knew they were not. Let us now consider what someone might be like to whom it had happened.

II

The Educated Person

THE "EDUCATED MAN" about whom so much talk is made remains an abstraction of small interest if he is nothing but teacher's pet, a typical creature of the educator's dream. Nevertheless, he is necessary to any discussion, for he is education's clearest end. That is why he should be treated with respect, in terms of his own nature. He is less a certain kind of man than he is any man who has become free to use the intellect he was born with: the intellect, and whatever else is important. And something is gained, as the sequel may suggest, by calling him not a man but a person.

He has been brilliantly defined, over and over again, in sentences whose brevity must be admired. He is one, for instance, "who knows what he is doing." This may claim too much for any mortal, but it aims in the right direction, as does the sister sentence which says he knows what he is saying. Alice never learned about that in the Wonderland which for us, if not for her, continues to be the best allegory of education. She never improved in the art of watching the words she used lest they be taken as referring to something different from the conventions she assumed; she never caught on to the fact that she might be as strange to others as others were to her; she got nowhere in the realm of possibility. "Why not?" was a rejoinder she failed to fathom.

The educated person, says Pascal, is one who has substituted learned ignorance for natural ignorance. That is valuable because it keeps ignorance in the picture, which otherwise would be false. "At home in the world"—the familiar phrase is a little too cozy for truth, though again it states the right desire; and it illuminates the image of aged persons blessed with the gift of occupation. For the last sign of education one can reveal is serenity in decrepitude, a sense that there is still something to be if not to do. Such persons in their prime had doubtless showed another sign: they could respect failure, or even idleness, if integrity came with it. And they were not too sure that they were judges of integrity, better and worse having been for them, as they surely are, big problems. "Those of us," remarked Rousseau, "who can best endure the good and evil of life are the best educated."

The list of insights is long. "An educated man is committed to reason—really committed." His habits are "the spirit of analysis and the perception of rule." He has, says William James, "a general sense of what, under various disguises, superiority has always signified and may still signify." He has learned, in other words from the same source, how to know a good man when he sees him. For Aristotle the educated man was one who had learned how to judge the competence of any teacher in any science. For Alexander Meiklejohn he is one "who tries to understand the whole of knowledge as well as one man can"; who is not discouraged by the legend that there is too much to know because he has kept faith with the principles of organization and analogy. More simply, he is one who knows how to read, write, speak, and listen—four major arts in which few are evenly proficient.

The educated person is free to disagree; and to agree. The first is now the more familiar act, so that many must believe it the sole proof of independence. Either can be proof, and both must be present before we acclaim the man. For only then are we convinced that he has taken truth for master.

"A cultivated intellect, because it is a good in itself, brings with it a power and a grace to every work and occupation which it undertakes." Thus Cardinal Newman, whom theology makes more lyric than the rest. He can invoke, with an ideality that is never absurd, a "clear, calm, accurate vision and comprehension of things, as far as the finite mind can embrace them, each in its place, and with its own characteristics upon it. It is almost prophetic from its knowledge of history; it is almost heart-searching from its knowledge of human nature; it has almost supernatural charity from its freedom from littleness and prejudice; it has almost the repose of faith, because nothing can startle it."

The path to this point, however, is thorny, and one has not arrived who was unwilling to be punished. "No one," says T. S. Eliot, "can become really educated without having pursued some study in which he took no interest—for it is a part of education to learn to interest ourselves in subjects for which we have no aptitude." The search for attractive studies—attractive, that is, before their true reward is comprehended—ends in the middle of a desert where distinction has been lost. The path has something puritan about it, something which the natural man resists in proportion to the very need he has for the happiness at its farther end.

That happiness consists in the possession of his own powers, and in the sense that he has done all he could to avoid the bewilderment of one who suspects he has missed the main thing. There is no happiness like this. Trust no philosopher who does not relish his existence and his thoughts.

His relish most recommends itself when it is hearty, and even when it is rude or alarming. It is not as if he had been led into a tomb. The educator's tone is sometimes that of one who asks the student to smile for the last time before he offers himself as a sacrifice to society. The voices of culture are too often dull, blank, and soundless; or else there is a sniffle and a whine suggesting that education is good for something else, not for its own sure self. At least one classic educator, Rabelais, was a roarer. And nobody can doubt the culture of John Jay Chapman in our time, even though he could write like this: "Is the education of the young the whole of life? I hate the young—I'm worn out with them. They absorb you and suck you dry and are vampires and selfish brutes at best. Give me some good old rum-soaked clubmen—who *can't* be improved and make no moral claims—and let me play checkers with them and look out of the club window and think about what I'll have for dinner."

The man who commands his mind may be as reckless as that: as apparently arrogant, as exultant over some secret glory which is in fact the source of his fascination. For the arrogance is only apparent, as becomes clear when we see how he refuses to boast about his education; he lets it recommend itself. It does this when we note that he is not weakly sensitive to the doubting word, to the slur at what is privately most precious to him. He can survive disagreement, just as he can weather unanimity.

Nor does he count on the whole world's becoming good day after tomorrow. This does not keep him from being glad that there are those today who would eradicate demonstrable ills. He even assists, for if he accepts evil he does not love it, and he is under no illusion that campaigns against inequality will mean the disappearance of injury between men. Reform for him does not cure evil so much as contain it in its native country, chance. He is perhaps the only man who can fight it without the illusion that it will stay away.

All this is high praise, and may seem to call for more than one man could be. But that is what education at the top does call for—each man becoming more than he is. A paradox emerges here. Pindar said that our chief duty consists in "becoming who we are." Were we not that already? What of the change that is supposed to take place in the educated person?

In an important sense he is not changed. He does not become, that is, a tiger or a crocodile. He becomes, we hope, only more human than he was. But he was already human. Then there are degrees of humanity, the last one yielding not the least but the most recognizable man, the person most clearly and completely a specimen of his kind. The more one changes in this way, the more one remains the same. The more, in other words, one becomes what one could be.

William Whewell avoided such tangles by saying blandly that the purpose of education is "to connect a man's mind with the general mind of the human race." And Comenius remarked with his wonderful simplicity: "Schools are the workshops of humanity." But the subject of man, always inseparable from the subject of education, remains difficult and obscure, with paradox at its heart because those who deal with it are themselves men. It was never more worth exploring than it is now, when so much that happens dehumanizes, and when there must be a corresponding hunger for knowledge of what after all the human is.

Our studies have not been taking this direction. As a philosopher has remarked, we think we know primitive man, Western man, the man of the Renaissance, the workingman, but we do not even pretend to know man, or what we mean when we say the word. Scott Buchanan once listed seven metaphors currently implicit in the term:

> Man is a system of electrons.
> Man is a machine.
> Man is an animal.
> Man is a bundle of habits.
> Man is a soul.
> Man is an angel.
> Man is divine.

There are those for whom all of these would be metaphors save one; there are others, perhaps, whose discourse builds itself upon two or more of them without consciousness of inconsistency. When we are metaphorical about something and do not know that we are, we prove that we have never examined it strictly. We confess, indeed, that we do not think it worthy of examination. But sooner or later, if the thing is man, our indifference counts against us.

Man's study of man is always threatened with frustration because it is the case of a species being measured by itself, which of course is not scientific. But man as philosopher, asking himself the further question, "What am I?", runs into as many difficulties. It is the oldest human question, and in our wisdom we have not answered it. Perhaps our wisdom, such as it is, appears in the fact that we have never been satisfied with an answer—or perhaps it should be said, never rested in a metaphor. We have continued to treat the problem as real: as one to which we do not know a simple solution. For all our present shallowness of thought about the matter, we do still recognize that man's distinguishing feature is his inability to know himself. He is a creature doomed to desire more knowledge, at least on this one point, than he will ever have. As a result he is both more than he need be and less than he would be. If he could slay his desire he might be content to exist rather than live. But he wants to live; and yet he never lives enough; that is, he never knows enough, for in proportion as he knows he lives. His predicament in the universe is probably peculiar. It is even noble. But it is a predicament, and this is no news to the educated person who has met it in every great writer he has read.

No wonder Gregory Nazianzen decided that "to educate man is the art of arts, for he is the most complex and mysterious of all creatures." Pascal called man "an incomprehensible monster . . . so necessarily mad that not to be mad would amount to another form of madness." Such language may sound extreme in an age which lets its metaphors go undetected because it supposes it has hold of the fact, because it rests in psychology and sociology. But it is not a dead language. Why man is both mind and body, and how they unite—these are questions we cannot afford to be too sure we have waved away. They have astonished and terrified great men.

To become more human than one was, therefore, is not in so far to find peace. It may be only then that the war begins, the war of understanding. William James never forgot that man is an animal with a tendency toward superfluity or excess; his wants are "fantastic and unnecessary." "Prune down his extravagance, sober him, and you undo him." He is a nervous animal, straining to comprehend what he contains, straining even to contain it. For it is bigger than he is. It is not an animal. "We must love a being who is in us," said Pascal, "and is not ourselves." This being in man goes by many names, serves under many metaphors. Whatever it is, its authority is huge, and one who has heard it speak will never be complacent again. It is something we inherit, and something into which we are educated. No one denies this, yet many seem to be unaware that the process is more like a revolution than it is like going to buy a new suit of clothes.

The educated person knows his own species as well as he can. But today he is at a disadvantage because he lacks a scale whereon to set the object of his examination. Too few other beings are available for comparison. There are the animals, whom we have with us whether or no; and we do use them for the purpose, frequently admiring the mirror more than our reflection in it. The comparison of men with animals, however, is at best a meager exercise. A richer field existed when there were gods and heroes, as with the Greeks, or God and the angels, as with the Christians. Without the idea of angels we have a poorer knowledge of that creature who once was lower than they, though he was higher than worm or ox. And since angels were still lower than God, and different from Him, the cloud of distinction thickened into something solid which intellectually we have lost.

Seeing man in a middle position between animals and angels lights up his dimensions as nothing else does. Animals are unconscious of their ignorance; angels know without difficulty. The middle creature, conscious of his ignorance, knows with difficulty. This makes him a more various creature than either of his neighbors, particularly since he is unstable enough in the category where he is suspended to yearn constantly for another. He tries to be brute or angel. Our language still permits us to denounce one who would be animal; "beast" is an epithet universally understood, along with the specifications of dog, hog, snake, lizard, cow, elephant, and cat. It is rarely, however, that a man these days is pitied for acting as if he thought he was an angel—a form of conduct, incidentally, which may make him more brute than before. Both mistakes are human. Man is the only being that can misconceive his nature. Animals do not conceive at all; angels conceive without effort or error.

Such a scale is one of man's most brilliant inventions; but our progress has been away from it. The thinner metaphors of animal and machine seem now to be all that we have, and even those are seldom recognized as functions of our speech. Perhaps there is no better explanation for the absence of irony in our art, or for the poor uses we make of poetry and history. Poetry is pretending, and history is something by which we prove that we could not have become other than what we are.

Man has a strange difficulty: he does not know what to be. No horse finds it hard to be a horse, or to know when he is one. He knows nothing else. And so, we assume, with angels—who know, however, what other things are, including man, though excluding God. What is it to be more of a man than one already is? It is not to grow taller, to have longer hair, to lose the body, to own the stars. Perhaps it is merely to know that such questions are important, and beset with perpetual difficulty. "We judge," said Pascal, "that animals do well what they do. Is there no rule whereby to judge men?" He thought there was. "To deny, to believe, and to doubt well are to a man what the race is to a horse."

To believe and doubt well. That is at least a program for the person whose perfection we have had in mind as the aim of education. Perfection, yet within the limits of his knowing nature. Those limits are harsh and final. There is nothing like them, however, in all the creature world. And let one distinction be clear. The individual is only a creature. The person has greater dignity. For he contains more than he is, and to the extent that he does so he appears to perform the miracle of being a part which possesses the whole.

The person in an individual is the man in him, the thing that politics respects when it is wise and good. It is what the doctrine of equality refers to. It is the medium through which individuals understand one another; it is the source of language and the explanation of love. And it solves many mysteries of the thing called personality. Individuality is less powerful; it is uniqueness, it is eccentricity, it is something we lack tongue to praise. He who is most a person is, strangely, the least personal of men; he is least hidebound by a notion he has of his own integrity. He is surprised when he hears of that, having all the while been occupied with the world's variety. There are many things he prefers to himself and tries to be. What he tries most steadily to be is a man. And when we praise him we praise his humanity. We compliment individuals; we praise persons for the virtues in them which they share with other men. An old way of saying this is that good men—that is, men—tend to be alike. Virtue is single and general; courage is not what one is but has.

Yet another mystery appears. For the possession of human virtues in high degree marks men, after all, so that they cannot be mistaken for their fellows. Personality is unique as individuality can never be. To say as much is to recognize for the last time that men are not angels. Their natures are rich with accident, and their animal base is profound. At the top, however, they touch a power which they hesitate to call their own.

The educated person is, then, a human being. As such he must cope with a special question which history never tires of asking. Does being human always mean the same thing? What of change? How long will the present last? For it is in the present that we know what we know. The completely educated person is one, we must suppose, who has settled some sort of relation in his mind between past, future, and present.

It is said to be more difficult now than ever before to be wise about these three. But it was always difficult, and we should not be in too much of a hurry to believe those who see change as something peculiar to our time. Such visionaries live in a perpetual panic. I have a friend who says he lives always at 11:59, waiting for the moment of midnight to strike the bell of utter change. And indeed the vast transformations now gathering in the world, the concentrations of public and private power, the appalling shrinkage of space, the increased impersonality of business and state, the multiplying artifices of life are not to be dismissed with a stare. The oil age is really new, and cities that now reach to the sky may soon be rotting in their riches. If history is the story of revolutions, another chapter may be nearing its last paragraph. Yet the student cannot leave it at that. And if he is a good student he will continue, under no matter what difficulties, his search for a center from which he can view both new and old. Such a center is the only place where the intellect can feel at home.

The priests of change are melancholy fellows who have little hope for the intellect. For them the human person is a butterfly that new shapes may crush just as it learns to lift its wings; education has other things to do than prepare a home for humanity; wherever it is built will be the wrong place; the tide of change sets always elsewhere; for education to perfect the powers of the person is only to make ready a sacrifice. So they mix their figures as they sweat to say the one thing they have in mind, namely, that the coming alterations are bound to come—so bound, indeed, as to make it doubtful that even an education in them is necessary, since soon we shall know all things without the trouble of thought. To such prophets it would be ridiculous to suggest that men need not be so ineffectual; that wisdom in at least a few persons might modify the future, which is among other things man's future.

The absolutists of the new are unaware that the present as they see it is "but an ambiguous sentence," says Jacques Barzun, "out of its context." The problem is one of reading —an art which they despise. The past, which they mistakenly identify as the sole concern of liberal education, puts them on the defensive. They think of it, in John Dewey's words, as "a rival of the present," and accuse the intellectual of wishing to make the present "an imitation of the past." The problem is immensely more complicated than that. The educated person recognizes no dry stretch between now and then. They are one river, and the more he knows about its length the better. He is a citizen of his age; but if he is a good citizen he studies the oldest laws as well as yesterday's statutes. He wants to know where things came from that neither he nor any contemporary invented. They may rejuvenate invention itself; an understanding of them may increase the rate of change fantastically beyond the dream of a provincial in time. The changes he wants are radical; they are improvements in persons. But to even the superficial ones he is not hostile. He assumes them with the flowing of the river, which he does not suppose will stop, as some reformers do, when one shift is made. If it could stop now it would have stopped before, and the shift would never have been possible. He is ready for shifts; but he does not forget that in proportion as the speed of alteration grows the need for memory deepens. No man can be wise enough. No man will be wise at all if he refuses to make the attempt.

The problem is the primeval one of permanence and change. Nobody but a fool teaches either that change does not occur or that there is nothing but change. An unassisted eye corrects the first error, and only a little tutoring is needed to see through the second. But no amount of education can remove the darkness from the theme, or can make it easy to know what in any particular case one should understand. The life of the mind would be simple if there were no change or if every change were total, for in neither instance would there be a problem; or it would have been solved millenniums ago, granting that without differences there would ever have been names, and that without names there would have been ideas.

The most familiar form of the problem has to do with the nature of man, concerning which the educated person will know what he knows about any nature, namely, that in so far as it is a nature it does not change. For then we should have another nature; meaning that in the case of man he would have another name. The reason we can keep on talking about man is that he changes but his nature does not; when he was ape he was not man, and as long as he is man he will not be angel. As long as man is, he does not alter beyond the recognition he first earned by being daily and yearly different. One who insists that human life changes has nevertheless spoken the words "human life" as if he knew what they meant. They meant for him the thing he could see changing. When, if ever, it becomes some other sort of life, he will cease to say it is human life that changes.

The educated person is neither scared by novelty nor bored without it. What can bore him is the bulletin which states that tomorrow nothing is going to be recognizable. Such bulletins are posted by people who know nothing of the past; or of the future, for if they considered what they were saying they would be silent, since it could not matter tomorrow what they had mouthed today. The worst nuisance, probably, is he who tolls the bell for good and evil and by some legerdemain of logic calls their passing good. The human spirit, however, is very tough; it can survive such f s, as it has survived the horrors, real or supposed, of its countless institutions.

Past, future, and present—they are three gods in one, and worship of them should be wisely distributed. The educated person knows one thing at least: the past is a burden which crushes only those who ignore it, and so do not study how to balance it on their shoulders. It is there in spite of everything; known and used for what it is, it can lighten the entire load. Dismissed from the mind by "practical" men, it can bring them to deserve Robert Maynard Hutchins's definition of them as "those who practice the errors of their forefathers."

"We never live," said Pascal, "but we hope to live; and, as we are always preparing to be happy, it is inevitable we should never be so." The poor student is lectured too much about another life for which this one of books and classes is preparing him; as if this one in itself were nothing, or could not be good. It is in fact one of the best lives available to men, some of whom childishly spend all their later years reliving it, as if none other followed. The educated person knows what it means to say that eternity is most like the present. It is now or never. It is the present in all its vastness that makes us serious, that makes us moral and religious. "The present," says Alfred North Whitehead, "contains all that there is. It is holy ground." And by some miracle it is ours alone—an amazing fact, to which history and prophecy are but footnotes. The educated person is no stranger to that mood in which Pascal once meditated:

When I consider the short duration of my life, swallowed up in the eternity before and after, the little space which I fill, and even can see, engulfed in the infinite immensity of spaces of which I am ignorant, and which know me not, I am frightened, and am astonished at being here rather than there; for there is no reason why here rather than there, why now rather than then.

III

Education for All

How many educated persons should there be? It is an old question which, in view of the exalted claims that have just been made for education, ought perhaps to change its form: How many can there be?

Nobody doubts that there should be as many as possible, but estimates of possibility range high and low, depending in every instance upon general theories which the speaker holds. Aldous Huxley, assuming madness in the mind of anyone who would "behave as though all human beings were by nature the same," proceeds at once to the proposition that it is "fantastic and absurd to give all children the same abstract, liberal education." Human beings, he explains, "belong to a variety of widely different types." This last is true enough, but it does not mean that they lack a common nature. If no such common nature exists, then the types have nothing to vary from except each other, and the word "education" as such loses its excuse for being. Men are alike and different, as Montaigne once made clear when he said that if the first were not true we should be unable to distinguish them from animals, and that if the second were not true we should be unable to tell them apart. Education has to master sameness and difference no less than permanence and change. The job is hard, and there is no short cut by way of denying our common nature. Knowledge of that is basic to all knowledge; it supplies the educator's first axiom: No human being should miss the education proper to human being. Either his differences from Tom and Harry are absolute, and so beyond the reach of any influence, or they are relative; in which latter case there is something that can and should be done about them.

Aldous Huxley calls liberal education abstract. If he means that it is general, or occupied with a nature assumed always to be the same, then he is right. He may mean something else: that liberal education is impractical and obscure. In these pages it is still to be defined, but when the moment comes for that it should already be clear that liberal education is nothing less than the complete education of men as men; it is the education of persons; or, ideally, it is education.

Albert Jay Nock has denied that more than a few men are so educable, for the same reason that only a few men are six feet tall: God saw fit to make them this way. Many men can be trained as animals, but only some can be educated in the great tradition which tells us most about our species. He attributes all the failures of American education to an interpretation of equality which makes it mean that the education of man should trim itself to the unassisted capacities of the average man, over whose head none of it should aim. We have assumed that "the whole subject-matter of education should be common property, not common in a true and proper sense, but, roughly, in the sense that so much of it as was not manageable by everybody should be disallowed and disregarded." There is no answer to that if "easily" is understood before "manageable." American education has been poor, not because it wanted to be universal but because it wanted to accomplish so little. The question is never how many are being educated, but how well the thing is being done. Educators, like magazine editors, persistently underrate the people. But the people in their turn have been at fault; they have expected from the most expensive system in the world more than they have required.

We should be sure we know what we mean when we say that certain persons cannot be educated. Strictly, this means that they have no minds. More often, and more loosely, it means that they do not show promise of being geniuses in a specialty—scientific, mathematical, or literary. Or it may mean no more than that a freshman in college has been discovered incompetent to read, write, and think. In the last case we might look up the elementary school from which the freshman came. As for geniuses, it is only God who makes some men sixteen feet tall. We should know whether or not our intention is to construe the statement strictly. If strictly, then we should have no student on our hands; years ago he would have been put among the defectives.

Education is for all, and there. can be no compromise with the proposition. "Just as in his mother's womb each man receives his full complement of limbs—hands, feet, tongue, etc.—although all men are not to be artificers, runners, scribes, or orators; so at school all men should be taught whatever concerns man, though in after life some things will be of more use to one man, others to another." Thus Comenius, the title page of whose *Great Didactic* promised that it would set forth "the whole art of teaching all things to all men"—to "the entire youth of both sexes, none excepted." It was a noble vision, and it has never been realized. We teach our entire youth, but we do not teach them enough.

What was once for a few must now be for the many. There is no escape from this—least of all through the sacrifice of quality to quantity. The necessity is not to produce a handful of masters; it is to produce as many masters as possible, even though this be millions. An ancient sentence about liberal education says it is the education worthy of a free man, and the converse is equally ancient: the free man is one who is worthy of a liberal education. Both sentences remain true, the only difficulty being to know how many men are capable of freedom. The capacity was once a favor bestowed by fortune: the gentleman was a rare fellow whose father was rich or famous. It is also, however, a capacity which nature bestows, and nature is prodigal. Liberal education in the modern world must aim at the generosity of nature, must work to make the aristocrat, the man of grace, the person, as numerous as fate allows. No society can succeed henceforth unless its last citizen is as free to become a prince and a philosopher as his powers permit. The greatest number of these is none too many for democracy, nor is the expense of producing them exorbitant. "A new degree of intellectual power," said Emerson, "is cheap at any price," and this is true no less for a country than for one of its citizens.

It might be feared that the price would be a depressing uniformity in institutions: so many colleges, so many filling stations. The fear is without foundation when education is responsible, and when there is general understanding that the common possession of it is the one bond of union in a

human world; and when this does not mean that cheap substitutes for it are assumed to be available. When all those
conditions exist, as now they do not, there is no danger of
mass production. When the end is the same, the means can
be different. It is only when we lack an end that we become
identical with one another in our confusion as to means.
Half measures are alike, substitutes are similar. If we do
not know what we want, we do not know how to be rivals
for it. The better and clearer our educational theory becomes, the more delightful will be the differences among
the institutions that apply it.

In proportion as the theory is clear it will not confound
itself with notions that the education of men, as distinguished from the training of animals, is something for a
class—say a leisure class. The only slaves in our society
ought to be its machines. There is a myth that machines
have minds and so are educable, but no man will admit this.
"We Americans," says Alexander Meiklejohn, "are determined that there shall not be in our society two kinds of
people. We will not have two kinds of schools—one for
gentlemen and ladies, the other for workers and servants.
We believe that every man and woman should be a 'worker.'
We believe that every man should be 'cultivated.' We believe that all men and women should govern. We believe
that all men and women should be governed. All the members of our society must have both liberal and vocational
education. There shall be one set, and only one set, of
schools for all people. The first postulate of a democracy
is equality of education. The gospel of Comenius is still
true." In proportion as our theory is clear it will agree with
the foregoing.

What, then, of the fact that education when liberal, when

occupied with human discipline, is arduous beyond all other known pursuits? Sufficient wisdom sometimes seems almost esoteric, an accomplishment of genius which the mass is bound to find unintelligible, no surface difference appearing between the subtlety of the philosopher and the caprice of the tyrant. Socrates supposed that philosophers would be useless only in a democracy, where he assumed they would not be heard. It is a question once more of the few and the many. And the answer is never that all men will be the best men. The sensible desire is simply that all men should be as good as possible. The higher the average the safer the state. But the pyramid will have symmetry only if the same attempt is made with every person: to produce in him the utmost of his humanity, on the assumption that this is what he possesses in common with every other person.

A democracy that is interested in its future will give each of its members as much liberal education as he can take, nor will it let him elect to miss that much because he is in a hurry to become something less than a man. It is obvious that all cannot be philosopher-kings, but it is just as obvious that all must not be less than they are; and a democracy must be prepared to give the entire quantity of itself that can be taken. The question must be asked in every case: How much? And the answer must be carefully considered.

Thomas Jefferson recommended a system of common schools for everybody and of universities for individual "geniuses raked from the rubbish." Matthew Arnold assumed that no society could thrive without universal and excellent elementary education; on top of which he would have built more and better secondary schools and universities than England had in his century. If the higher institutions were not for all, Arnold's order of education at least provided in the case of any man a "bar or condition" between him and what he aimed at. The bar was there for the public safety, ensuring that wolves did not creep into the fold. In our day it is recognized by such a champion of universal education as Robert Maynard Hutchins that in the early stages a distinction appears between those whose training should continue to be general and those who are so exclusively "hand-minded" as to suggest the wisdom of drawing them off into manual or technical schools. At a higher level he consents to the choice between a college and a technical institute. At the highest level, the university level, he restricts education "to those who have demonstrated their ability to profit by it."

Such proposals differ in detail, and yet something is constant in them: the conviction that people should be taught as long as possible in terms of their likeness to one another, and that when differences of ability emerge, not to say differences of genius, the highest training should be free for those who deserve it, and only for those. All indeed is free, at the same time that all is as sound as the best thought about education can make it. The details matter less than the principle. In England it has been proposed that public education cease at fourteen so that boys and girls may depart into adult life with the idea that when they are indeed adult they shall be privileged to return, as Danes do to their People's High Schools, and be willing students of permanent things. The variety of plans only attests the constancy of the conviction that under democracy education must be as wide as the world.

But now as to democracy. The term is central to any modern theory of education; so much so that it can be fatal if misused. Its most frequent misuse consists in saying that education must devote all of its energies to elucidating and defending the democracy in force today. Its best use would consist in saying that education, having the same end as democracy, can best serve human good by perfecting itself.

The discussion goes on in a political crisis that is world-wide and perilous, so that hurry of thought and the resort to slogans are not to be wondered at. But in human history there has seldom been a greater need for slow, deep thinking on a level comparable to that which theology once dominated. "Man is naturally a political animal," said Aristotle; politics for him was a nobler and more divine ethics, a science permitting the fullest statement of man's good. If this was a figure then, circumstances have made it almost literal now, when democracy seems to be the only heir of religion, and the only existing agent of its educational function. This is crucial, for it reminds us that the young person being educated has every right to ask what he is going to so much trouble for. Why is he being coaxed to train his mind? Toward what sort of citizenship, in what society? And if not in the City of God, then what is meant by the City of Man? Is it something which deserves that he should study for its sake to become better than himself? Education must have answers to such questions. So in these times must democracy, which is our only educator possessing full authority.

Answers are not easy, granted that they are possible, for the simple reason that man prefers a lever if he is to lift himself. A lever, and then a fulcrum at least as good as God was in another age of faith. "Our society," said Matthew Arnold, "is probably destined to become more democratic; who or what will give a high tone to the nation then?" This is the question that ought to keep statesmen and educators awake. They may imagine, for instance, religion embodied in a world state whose officials are all but priests—all but Lincolns—because its purpose is more than "merely" political. But what is to prevent the propagation of specious faiths, usable by ruthless individuals for their private ends? What of the "political religions" which now endanger even our most elementary liberties? How is the citizen to distinguish? He is prepared to distrust a demagogue who does not disguise his ambition; he is ill prepared to recognize a prophet, for the language of prophecy is not in good repute. And he is as impotent as men have ever been to arrive at a definition of justice that fits itself precisely to the present scene. In heaven, yes, or in the realm of ideas. But here among the rival claims of persons and parties it is harder to be certain.

The citizen, if he is serious, has probably begun to suspect that nothing less than wisdom and virtue will solve the important political and economic problems of his or any other time. And he may have decided that he is willing to recognize some state which will prove that it is above class or sect, that it seeks both public and private justice, that its hope is to unite temperance with courage in wise minds both famous and obscure. He would have no fear of such a state, knowing that all it feared was his own failure to be strong and good. He would gladly serve it, believing that he thereby served his own best self. Politics is never sound when the citizen fears the state—when the only freedom he wants is freedom from it. Freedom in it is the happier desire.

Plato in his *Laws* remarked that the most important officer in a state would be its minister of education. Such a minister, we know, can be disastrously important. It is right to fear a state, even a democratic one, which takes the short cut to its citizens and issues them articles of unexamined belief. It is not how much they believe that matters, it is how well they think; and a democracy which is unwilling that they should think well, no matter what they think, does not trust itself. The best thought serves it best.

The recent situation in America, when it appeared that young people believed nothing at all, was a supporting case, not for the theory that democracy should be an instrument of indoctrination but for the theory that thought is indispensable. For the failure of the young people in question was the failure to believe in the necessity of thought. What they did believe was that all statements are probably untrue, and that it is scarcely worth while to labor at discovering whether some are less so than others. This was believing, not thinking; their failure was the failure to think well. The excuse has been offered that society had spoiled them by permitting commercial agencies and groups of special pleaders to prevail; the education of youth had slipped by default into the hands of those who were bound to discredit education itself, and democracy with it. The accusation has point. Practically, it means that the schools and colleges should have done a better job. But a better job of what? Not of advertising democracy in its present degree, not of setting up little communities to ape the current practice as though that were final. The disease was real, but the remedy is not to make democracy another special pleader. It cannot afford to plead for less than the use by the student of his whole mind, no matter where it takes him. It ought to take him in the direction of more democracy than we have. Which is what the democracy we have should desire, and does desire in proportion as it is pure.

What the student does not want to feel is that he is being used, even by a democracy that thinks itself perfect. "A state which dwarfs its men in order that they may be more docile instruments in its hands even for beneficial purposes will find that with small men no great thing can really be accomplished." The warning of John Stuart Mill has lost no force. The good state wants great democrats; and gets them by teaching the love of truth; and teaches that by teaching the importance of thinking well. It does not achieve its end by pretense or coercion, or by a conspiracy to confuse the attempt with the deed. "There is no such thing," says Albert Jay Nock, "as democratic manners; manners are either bad or good." So with anything else that is human. There is no such thing as democratic morals and ideas. Morals are either bad or good; ideas are either shallow or profound. Democracy's business is with morals as such, and with the deepest ideas available to its citizens.

It has been said that the question is not what education can do for democracy but what democracy can do for education. If democracy is not strong enough to deserve the compliment implied, it is not strong enough to teach. Democracy as educator is man teaching. It serves itself by making its pupils free—not free from or for the state, but absolutely free. This is another way of saying that it serves itself by making men. But education too has the job of making men. So education is democracy, and democracy is education. The statesman is a teacher, and the teacher is a statesman. There is no such thing as education for democracy. Education is either bad or good. The best education makes the best men; and they will be none too good for democracy.

Democracy cannot survive a loss of faith that the best

man will make the best citizen. It certainly cannot afford to educate men for citizenship, for efficiency, or for use. Its only authority is reason, just as its only strength is criticism. It will not distinguish between its own good and the happiness of its members. It will study how to distribute well the things that are good for men, but it will study with equal care the goods of men, which incidentally make more sense in the singular: the good of man. The citizen will never forgive a society, democratic or otherwise, which taught him to do what time has shown to be wrong or silly. He can never blame a society which encouraged him to be all that he could be. If the teaching was good, he has no one else to blame. Democracy does not provide alibis.

The circle of the relation between the state and the individual, a circle which is drawn when we say that each depends upon the other for its good, can be broken only if we distinguish between the individual and the person. The individual has no relation to anything except the state or society of which he is a member, and to which he is relative. But the person is not a member. He is the body of himself, and as such is always to be understood as an end, not a means. As a ruler, he has first ordered his own soul. As the ruled, he likewise orders his soul. And this is something which he is unique among creatures in knowing how to do, even though he may never do it perfectly. The good state—democracy—will let him try, on the theory that good citizenship will follow naturally from even moderate success; though it will let him try anyway. For without autonomy he cannot find the center in himself from which in fact emanate the very generosity and lawfulness, the respect for others that is a form of respect for himself, necessary to the operation of society at all. Society may command fear and obedience; it cannot force love or friendship, which are irreducibly personal, and developed in places to which politics as most conceive it has no access. Yet they are the foundation of good politics, which in this sense must be personal to succeed greatly. Democracy wants millions of one-man revolutions, if only because the result might be a nation of persons worth organizing. Norman Foerster has suggested that "the individual, while learning to live wisely, becomes progressively more fit to be lived with." He supports the remark with a line from Aeschylus: "The wise have much in common with one another." The only common good is that which is common to good men.

The powers of the person are what education wishes to perfect. To aim at anything less is to belittle men; to fasten somewhere on their exterior a crank which accident or tyrants can twist to set machinery going. The person is not machinery which others can run. His mind has its own laws, which are the laws of thought itself. A congressman recently recommended that American youth be "taught how to think internationally." It would be still better to teach them how to think. Democracy depends for its life upon the chance that every man will make all the judgments he can. When he falls short of that he gives his government another name. He is no longer at home in the republic of the mind, where, since thought is free and only merit makes one eminent, he is less than a slave.

The state is doubtless superior to the individual on many counts. But when the question is one of good or bad, right or wrong, true or false, democracy must appeal to insight, imagination, and judgment; and these are personal things— things, that is, of man rather than of society. By personal, it should be clear, the eccentric is not signified. Insight into what? Imagination about what? Judgment concerning what? Not, surely, the accidents of individual belief, but the essentials of the human situation. The individual, thinking well about these, becomes personal in the grand dimension. The trivial dimension is something with which we happen to be more familiar, but this should not discourage us from using the word, which has a long and important history. To be personal in the trivial dimension means that in politics we cultivate little areas of freedom where we can live in isolation from the wilderness of compulsion. We have secrets; we lead the buried life. The large area of human freedom is a better place to breathe in. It is a general area, and in it some of our license is lost. But it is the only region where personality is finally possible. For the paradox once more emerges: an individual, thinking the best thoughts of which he is capable, and mastering the human discipline without jealousy for his own rule, becomes more of himself than he was before. "Certain men," wrote Plato in one of his letters, "ought to surpass other men more than the other men surpass children." If that is a definition of aristocracy, the definition of democracy would be a condition in which all men surpass themselves, putting behind them childish things.

Democracy when it is secure will not deny its inferiority to persons. The superiority of its persons is its only strength. To say as much is to say that democracy lives dangerously. For humanity is dangerous, and is not to be controlled by committees of men. But the danger from its freedom—from a program which asks it what it can be rather than tells it what to do—is less than the blind risk that is run when the program is to mislead and miseducate it; or, what amounts to the same thing, to educate it partially. No risk

is as real as that. There is danger anyway, as all teachers
of pupils and parents of children know. Good teachers, parents, and states, however, will prefer the high danger to
the low.

"The question, 'What is a good education?'," says Mortimer Adler in a summary that must be borrowed here, "can
be answered in two ways: either in terms of what is good
for men at any time and place because they are men, or in
terms of what is good for men considered only as members
of a particular social or political order. The best society
is the one in which the two answers are the same." That
best society, doubtless, is still to exist on earth. But when
it completely exists, perhaps at the end of history, its name
will be democracy. And all of its citizens will be educated
persons.

IV

Liberal Education

A LIBERAL education is more than a classical education, more than an education in English literature, more than an education in what is called "the humanities," and more than a training in the moral virtues. Each of these is necessary to the whole, but it is not the whole; nor, as education is conducted today, is it a large part. Ideally the part of each is very large, and subsequently this should be clear. For the present it must suffice to consider all four things as the inadequate disciplines which in practice they are.

An education in the literatures of Greece and Rome—particularly Greece—ought to be a great thing. But for centuries it has been less than that, and a few years ago it was possible for Alfred North Whitehead to say, finally and funereally: "Of all types of man today existing, classical scholars are the most remote from the Greeks of the Periclean times." Since those were the supreme times of Western intellect and art, the implication is that the cord between past and present has been cut. Not cut completely; but few would deny that a loss has been sustained, or that if it ever became total, barbarism would be on its way back.

Greek literature is not everything, yet it is the heart of what we need to know, along with Roman literature, its derivative. The Greek and Latin languages, also indispensable to our knowledge, are another matter. Our failure has consisted in confusing the relation between a right study of the literatures and a right study of the languages. Literature, to be brief, has been studied as language, and ever more narrowly. The worst result has been hatred of Greek and Latin, and a prevailing ignorance of what they once were used for. They were used to give an account of the world, the clearest and the grandest that we have. Their study has dwindled to a literary piddling which, when philological, has a limited value; when esthetic, it has less value still.

A generation ago Frank Moore Colby observed that those who congratulated themselves in the press upon their classical educations—the classics, as usual, being under fire—were singularly inhumane. " 'Philonous' and 'Scientificus' come out about even in dullness, and when old 'Philomathicus' writes from Warwickshire about all that Virgil has done for him, everyone with a grain of good taste is sorry Virgil did it. To the mind of an impartial witness it always ends in a draw. If they did not brag about it, you could no more tell which of them had had the classics and which had not, than you could tell which was vaccinated, if they did not roll up their sleeves. The only thing you can make out of the affair, with scientific certainty, is that in every case either the education was wrong or the wrong man was educated. . . . Men turn to the classics in the hope of meeting precisely the sort of people who would not write these articles on the classics."

So low a degree of fame is likely to be the fate of any

educational discipline when it becomes a specialty, and science might remember this. But few specialties have ever sunk to the level indicated by Colby, himself a lover of the classics. And even classical studies had not been denounced in the preceding century as dull; they were said to be silly. "There is perhaps no sight in the world," thought Huxley, "more saddening and revolting than is offered by men sunk in ignorance of everything but what other men have written; seemingly devoid of moral belief or guidance; but with the sense of beauty so keen, and the power of expression so cultivated, that their sensual caterwauling may be almost mistaken for the music of the spheres." This might be dismissed as the prejudice of a scientist. But the literary Newman could approve a criticism of classical education which charged that it "trains up many young men in a style of elegant imbecility utterly unworthy of the talents with which nature has endowed them. . . . A classical scholar of twenty-three or twenty-four is a man principally conversant with works of imagination. His feelings are quick, his fancy lively, and his taste good. Talents for speculation and original inquiry he has none, nor has he formed the invaluable habit of pushing things up to their first principles, or of collecting dry and unamusing facts as the materials for reasoning. All the solid and masculine parts of his understanding are left wholly without cultivation; he hates the pain of thinking, and suspects every man whose boldness and originality call upon him to defend his opinions and prove his assertions."

Both Huxley and Newman, let it be noted, assume of classical education that all it does is acquaint the student with the "beauties" of two literatures. The suggestion is that such authors as Plato, Aristotle, Euclid, Hippocrates, and the great historians, and even the epic and dramatic poets on their ethical side, which means in their philosophical aspect, are somehow missed. The suggestion is fair, and can be reinforced. It might be something to acquaint the student with only a little less than that full beauty which our most masculine wisdom is required to understand when we really read Homer or Sophocles. Not even that, however, has been regularly done. Sometimes the beauty has not been there at all. The study has been of lines as lines, of constructions as constructions. The discipline has been in languages, and not for their gold but for the ordinary metal with which this is mixed. The great writers have not been read greatly.

The failure over all has been the failure to see these writers either in the setting of their life or in that of ours, which is substantially the same. Literature is a means to something bigger than itself; it makes the world available to us as chance and appetite do not. Any study of Greek and Roman literature can be rewarding, but the study of it cannot be final if we do not consider the end to which it was and is so magnificent a means. What is it in fact about? Why should we be stricken with intellectual and spiritual poverty if we lost all memory of it? Is it truly necessary for us to know what it says? The student who has no answers to these questions, either because he has never been moved to think about them or because he has the impression that only archaeologists know that sort of thing, has not been educated, classically or otherwise.

The situation shows signs of improving, now that we are permitted to read this literature in translation and thus to mingle its stream with such other streams of knowledge as flow under our thought. It may again become something like the common and familiar possession which in theory, if never quite in practice, it once was. But it still has distances to go. And it still has to find its right place among a number of other things necessary for our education.

A liberal education is so much more than what passes today as an education in English that the following words of I. A. Richards seem weirdly unreal: "We teachers of English have a great responsibility. We are the guardians of the main channel through which has come down to us whatever is high-hearted, courageous, noble, and passionate in its hopes for man, whatever is faithful, whatever is honorable, whatever is serious and sincere, whatever is most aware of man's nature and his fate, whatever is most ready to uphold and defend it." That is fine, but few teachers of English deserve it. Even if they performed all that their subject made possible they would not be sufficient agents of a liberal education; English literature, great as it is, is less than enough for the purpose. What is meant by calling it "the main channel" through which everything good comes down to us? Platonism in English poetry brings along no more than one per cent of Plato. The question at hand, however, is not so much the importance of English literature as the efficacy of the teaching that prevails in its name.

Much that Huxley and Newman said about classical studies could be said about English studies. It is seldom that the great books in English are greatly read. This is partly because lesser books, on the mistaken theory that they are easier, are preferred; in such a case the great ones are not read at all. It is partly, however, because the teachers lack understanding of what literature at its best can be about. It can be about almost everything, but the student is rarely informed of this. A teacher may be pardoned for not being a genius at criticism, and for failing therefore to render a perfect account of the artistic triumph before him. It is more difficult to pardon him when he dodges in discussion the themes of good and evil, God and man, true and false, large and small, the same and the different. Success on both levels is proper to the full analysis of art, and the teacher would be a better critic of effects if he were better trained as a critic of ideas. But a peculiar genius is required in the first case, whereas an educated humanity is sufficient in the second.

When this is absent, the reason is likely to be that the teacher himself has been taught English literature rather than literature. There is an important difference between the two. If English literature is great, it is great as literature. But of what does such greatness consist, and in how many other places can it be found? It is not universally required of English students that they know Greek literature; a doctor of philosophy can be ignorant of Homer. This makes him provincial, and it leaves him embarrassed when he is called upon to be serious and sincere, whether in his judgment of a modern masterpiece or in his discourse concerning the fundamentals, philosophical and moral, in which humanity is trained. The student is naturally more interested in those fundamentals than he is in anything else, since the young are incorrigibly moral. The usual thing is to shame him out of this, lest he be a prig. What he was trying to do was grow up.

If there is merit in the proposal that English departments be abolished in favor of departments which shall have literature in the large as their concern—and ultimately that all departments be abolished, but this is something to be dis-

[48]

cussed in another connection—the reason is not that English literature is a little thing, but that it is taught as such. It has become a specialty; that is, a subject the importance of which no one is educated to know. The advanced study of it today is a scandal too seldom denounced. Students improve their knowledge not of it but about it. The "sheer science" of it as a subject "can be and often is mastered," says Albert Jay Nock, "by one who is completely lacking in its spirit or in comprehension of its content." This can mean either that such a man is helpless when he is face to face with it as art or childish when he has to say what it is about.

Literary scholarship as we know it is most at home among the small books it can explain, the imperfect ones that have palpable sources in other books. The great books whose source is all books and all life are not to be explained so easily; and none of them can be explained away. Many professors of English behave as though they would like to explain literature away; that, for them, would be mastering it. The error lies in their own education, which probably was not an education even in the works of one great writer. If all students of English were set to studying Shakespeare, who is so much the greatest of English writers that this might be no more than simply sensible, the result could be, in the first place, a generation of teachers who knew their business; it could be, in the second place, a striking advance in our knowledge of Shakespeare. There are no signs at the moment that such a project would be considered anything but insane.

English as a language gains nothing, either, by being the business of a department. It seems to have been better taught when everybody taught it. For it has to do with the arts of reading and writing, and those are arts that all must know, based as they are upon the grammar, the logic, and the rhetoric which anywhere make thought and expression possible, and which everywhere should be the concern of teachers. As things stand they are left to the teacher of English; who, however, has as little love for logic as he has patience with grammar, and who in the average case shares the contemporary view that rhetoric is vulgar. Nothing more need be said here about the weakness of teachers for making reading easy the hard way—that is, the dull and unrewarding way of inferior books, even of textbooks to which the classics are "supplementary."

A current expedient designed to eke out the meager living offered by English and the classics is fine as far as it goes. Courses in "the humanities," or departments and divisions of them, flourish widely across America, and their scope is intelligently generous. Not only the great literary works of Greece, Rome, and England, but their European companions in other languages—the books of Dante, Machiavelli, Rabelais, Montaigne, Cervantes, Spinoza, Molière, Pascal, Racine, Voltaire, Rousseau, and Goethe—become the materials for a view of man's long intellectual achievement. And such is the virtue of this expedient, so instantaneous is its success wherever it is tried, that some suppose it has given us liberal education at one stroke. The result is often referred to, indeed, as the corrective which was needed in a system dominated by science. The sciences were too much admired for knowing clearly what they wanted to do, for being masters of the arts proper to their conduct. Now letters, it is said, are also to have their headquarters on the main thoroughfare. Letters, with as much philosophy as the student can take, and with history serving as always somewhere in the rear; the fine arts, too, lurking in such crevices of the structure as its planners leave open for the purpose. This, a prevailing impression has it, is the liberal education that will supplement science, and so save the spirit of man intact against the threats to it of nature methodized.

But liberal education is not everything except science; it is not a remnant of "other things" toward which we must be pious. If science is master of the intellectual arts proper to the conduct of its affairs, then science is liberal too; and letters should learn from it how to be something better than the extra, the additional, the amateur army they now seem to be. Science has no doubt of its importance. Letters must have, or they would not speak of themselves as "also important." Perhaps they can learn from science how to take care of themselves. In the long run this might mean that they would know how to take care of science.

Their intrinsic importance is so great that their champions in "the humanities" are of course correct in insisting that they are necessary rather than nice. Poetry, story, and speculation are more than pleasant to encounter; they are indispensable if we would know ourselves as men. To live with Herodotus, Euripides, Aristotle, Lucretius, Dante, Shakespeare, Cervantes, Pascal, Swift, Balzac, Dickens, or Tolstoy—to take only a few names at random, and to add no musicians, painters, or sculptors—is to be wiser than experience can make us in those deep matters that have most closely to do with family, friends, rulers, and whatever gods there be. To live with them is indeed experience of the essential kind, since it takes us beyond the local and the accidental, at the same moment that it lets us know how uniquely valuable a place and a time can be.

The error is to ape science, in so far as science makes claims for its exclusive importance, by making equivalent claims for literature. Neither is exclusively important, and when it says so it does not understand the other. Nor will it be able to defend itself if and when it has to.

Every educator knows how Matthew Arnold in the last century turned to literature as a substitute for the religion which had been lost. But Arnold's conception of the matter has been narrowly reported. He did not recommend the study of poetry as something merely additional to science. These words of his should be examined: "We shall find that this art, and poetry, and eloquence, have in fact not only the power of refreshing and delighting us, they have also the power—such is the strength and worth, in essentials, of their authors' criticism of life—they have a fortifying, and elevating, and quickening, and suggesting power, capable of wonderfully helping us to relate the results of modern science to our need for conduct, our need for beauty." The particular word to be noted is "relate." Arnold's own education was not complete, and it cannot be claimed for him, nor did he ever claim for himself, that he knew how to relate science to conduct. Yet he did perceive that the lost religion was something vast and solid to which both science and poetry had been servants.

In his own practice as critic and prophet he was limited to the vision of ancient letters as valuable to modern men because they were a sort of backlog in barren times, a reservoir of feelings and ideas which, for the very reason that they had been conceived in the context of divine or permanent good, might now assist humanity to assert its greatness. Arnold saw humanity not as animal but as moral. The animal achieves his comfort by cunning, to adopt

Stuart Sherman's paraphrase, but man as a moral being
seeks only to perfect his essence. He is small in space and
time, but his soul is indefinably large, and his powers are
more than analytical or investigative; they are sensitive
too, they put themselves forth in search of the best in conduct, beauty, and manners. Arnold was limited by a literary
education. He was not a perfect liberal artist, as to be sure
no man will ever be. He did not, however, lose sight of
relations; he suggested that the program of education is
not to discover which of the two things, science and art, is
paramount, but how they should be understood as statements, ideally considered, of the same fact.

And by literature he did not mean belles-lettres. No one
can forget how important he found poetry to be. But some
have forgotten that he meant by knowing Greece "knowing
her as the giver of Greek art, and the guide to a free and
right use of reason and to scientific method, and the founder
of our mathematics and physics and astronomy and biology
—I understand knowing her as all this, and not merely knowing certain Greek poems, and histories, and treatises, and
speeches." So with the modern nations. "I mean not merely
knowing their belles-lettres, but knowing also what has
been done by such men as Copernicus, Galileo, Newton,
Darwin."

If we are looking for a weakness in Arnold's position,
the word to note is "also." He still was not the man to say
how the relations he had imagined should be explored. He
still could say on another page that literature contains "the
materials which suffice for making us know ourselves and
the world." It is dangerous to believe this, for it is not true.
It is particularly dangerous to the study and the practice
of letters. For books even at their literary best are only half

of the liberal tradition. Without wisdom in the other half, which we label mathematics and science, they tend to become in our hands, as a philosopher has warned, "empty and romantic." It is then that we grow hysterical in our claims for them. It is then that we become worse enemies of books than science has ever been.

A legend persists that science is not humane, and less than nothing is done to scotch it when departments of "the humanities" are set over against departments of "the sciences." Even when they are set alongside, with no intention of rivalry or hostility, the fact of the separation is more eloquent than any excuse for it could be. By science, of course, is not meant the technological religions which now fight one another for a following. Science is knowledge, and knowledge cannot be inhumane.

The Greeks were scientists, as Arnold agreed with Huxley in saying. Huxley, anticipating Whitehead, thought that the limitation of the humanists in his day consisted in their having not too much of the Greek spirit but too little of it. "We cannot know all the best thoughts and sayings of the Greeks unless we know what they thought about natural phenomena. We cannot fully apprehend their criticism of life unless we understand the extent to which that criticism was affected by scientific conceptions. We falsely pretend to be the inheritors of their culture unless we are penetrated, as the best minds among them were, with an unhesitating faith that the free employment of reason, in accordance with scientific method, is the sole method of reaching truth." If the end of the last sentence betrays its writer as one for whom science is a sufficient religion, and if later on he takes the same tone in conciliating letters that Arnold had taken in conciliating science—"nevertheless, I am the last person to question the importance of genuine literary education, or to suppose that intellectual culture can be complete without it"—so that he too takes his place among those whom relations baffle, it remains obvious that he touches traditional humanism at its weakest point. He is the traditional scientist in doing so, and neither tradition is adequate to the human need. Science and art have to understand, not conciliate, each other. But in his measure he is right. Letters alone are no better as a religion than the science is which troubles us with its claims.

To the extent that "the humanities"—an unfortunate term—are merely rewarming "humanism"—another unfortunate term—they will take us only part way to a liberal education. For humanism was never good enough. It took too thin a view of man. It separated him from nature as the Greeks had never done. The process began in Rome, which loved Hellenic literature not wisely but too well, taking it as scripture and permitting rhetoricians to select even from that scripture the purely literary portion. This was the portion, thought Rome, that had to do properly with man; this was the learning a noble person might possess. When noble meant highborn, learning meant accomplishment—the badge by which one showed that one was free. It was an external ornament, classical education signifying the education of a class. As snobbery this does not concern us, but as a theory of education it does, for it indicates how much is lost when man falls in love with the top of his mind.

The humanism of the Renaissance was still further denatured. The Renaissance had its science as Rome had not, but John Dewey has put the matter compactly: "The philosophy which professed itself based upon science . . . was

[55]

either dualistic in character, marked by a sharp division between mind (characterizing man) and matter, constituting nature; or else it was openly mechanical, reducing the signal features of human life to illusion. In the former case, it allowed the claims of certain studies to be the peculiar consignees of mental values, and indirectly strengthened their claim to superiority, since human beings would incline to regard human affairs as of chief importance at least to themselves. In the latter case, it called out a reaction which threw doubt and suspicion upon the value of physical science, giving occasion for treating it as an enemy to man's higher interests. . . . Thus the immediate effect of modern science was . . . to establish the physical and the humanistic studies as two disconnected groups." The mutual mystery of physics and philosophy, or biology and art, is therefore centuries old, and a modern university in which scientists and poets know nothing about each other but recapitulates the fable of a divorce. The result is more ignorance on both sides than we can do with.

Neither side is to be chosen as if there were a legitimate dispute between them, since there is not; but one who is called upon to judge whether mind or matter is the better object of discipline today, as things go in institutions of learning, has to say that it is matter. The science we use liberates more minds than the classics we have, since we do not know how to use the classics. And the reason we do not know their use is that we read them in isolation. The scientist has his isolation too, and it is ugly; but the solitude of the humanist is insignificant. It is not, to recall Newman's words, solid or masculine. The humanist makes claims for his books which nobody is bound to recognize. He may shame us occasionally with the thought that we are not "fine." enough, but we observe that he is only fine, and we know that to be only fine is to be less than a man can be.

The humanist suffers most in our estimation when he fails to convince us that he has a discipline. The discipline of science may be narrow, but it is real. The study of literature is not rigorous enough to be real. Criticism has its victories no less than investigation. But the laws by which they are won are hard laws; they are the rules of an art, or a set of arts, which the humanist has forgotten. His worst enemy is not the chemist or the engineer, it is himself if he has forgotten that knowledge in his domain can be as exact as it is anywhere. Perhaps more exact, though if he knew what that meant he would be a philosopher. He is too literary because he is not philosophical enough. But even the philosophers of the time maintain a solitude which assists us little in the game of understanding. It has been claimed that education will recover its full human stature when the humanities, meaning literature and philosophy, once more are dominant. If the humanities are nothing but humanism as we have known it, their dominance will be no better than that of the ribboned hat which mistakes itself for the head. Education prefers to be dominated by humanity. Man is in the same breath metaphysician, philosopher, scientist, and poet. If he is also numbskull and genius, education has to admit that it cannot cope with those.

One further question requires to be asked before the meaning of liberal education can be clear. It has to do with the virtue, or the virtues, of an educated person. Much difference is made by our decision here between the singular and the plural. All of the virtues may ultimately be one, but it has been helpful to distinguish and name them as if they were several. To do so enriches understanding, makes it evident that we know our nature, and renders possible a sort of order in the pursuit of its perfection.

A traditional classification discovers four kinds of virtue: the vegetative or physical, belonging to a sound and graceful body; the moral, suggesting an ordered soul; the intellectual, proving the possession of a mind disciplined to do whatever mind can do; and the theological, preparing us for citizenship in eternity. It should be admitted right away that all of these kinds depend upon one another—even, perhaps, the first and the fourth. Nobody has been successful in separating one sort and making it absolute. Yet a current emphasis upon character as the aim of education means that the moral virtues are in process of preferment, and demands that we pause at this place to consider what such an emphasis means. The moral virtues are being preferred to the intellectual virtues. The first and fourth kinds scarcely enter the discussion, for two reasons that are not identical. A sound body is almost everywhere assumed to have a part equally in moral and in intellectual health. And the theological virtues are unfashionable.

It is said today with impressive regularity that schools and colleges must take over moral education because the home, the church, and society in general have ceased to be its agents. The typical student, it is urged, comes from a community that is morally and emotionally barren. Business is more and more impersonal, and therefore progressively unmoral. The people lack spontaneous folk rituals which bring them together in fruitful work or play; they assemble only along the production belt, or in silent rows of darkened seats, passively watching movies. When they go home it is to a bleakness such as no former world has known. Children rarely know the details of what their fathers do, and so are not moved to the moral exercise of imitating them. Emerson's picture of family life is as archaic as the age of the patriarchs: "The household is a school of power. There, within the door, learn the tragicomedy of human life. Here is the sincere thing, the wondrous composition for which day and night go round. In that routine are the sacred relations, the passions that bind and sever. Here affections glow, here the secrets of character are told."

We are told we can no longer take for granted that society sends its young to school with a common body of usable precepts. They do not come sharing universal notions of right and wrong, good and bad, the becoming and the unbecoming. The Greek philosophers could count on a quick and natural understanding of what they meant by "right reason." It was the prevailing morality, of which we have no equivalent. Mankind's "most precious instrument of progress, the impracticable ethics of Christianity," is no longer a tool in hand. A hundred years ago in America the parents of a boy could cheerfully send him to college for an intellectual education because they knew they had given him its moral base. Now they send him for the second thing alone, or at any rate first. And this is why, the doctrine goes on to insist, we must not be too narrow in our resolution to make education intellectually better. Granted that it has not been good enough in this way, the error would be to suppose that it can be so. The very extracurricular antics which we ridicule are nothing but the attempts of students to provide themselves with a full life at last. Let education be church and home, let character be built on the campus.

But it is not as simple as that. To agree with Plato that "education makes men good," and with Aristotle that "no one would say a man was happy who had no fortitude, no temperance, no justice, no prudence," is not at once to de-cide that the prime conscious occupation of the teacher can ever be with character. "A man's character is his fate," said Heraclitus, and William James, extending the state-ment, fixed it as certain that "all our life is but a mass of habits systematically organized for our weal or woe, and bearing us irresistibly toward our destiny." The moral vir-tues, St. Augustine remarked, are "the proper use of our freedom." Then the moral virtues, and the character we connect them with, are of high importance. But there is that word "freedom," which requires the intellect for its proper understanding; and there is the known difficulty of taking the moral virtues by direct assault.

Socrates, who loved virtue as much as any man, is famous among other reasons because he said that it could not be taught. It can be loved; and the tension among our various desires—to be temperate, to be courageous, to be wise—can issue in a harmony which Socrates best knew how to praise; but the moral virtues are beyond precept. Education is vitally concerned with them, but it does not give "courses in character." For one thing, as Aristotle insisted in the opening pages of his *Ethics*, age and experience are neces-sary; young men have not lived long enough to know why temperance and wisdom are good. Principles can be memo-rized, but their meaning waits upon their application—itself perhaps the most difficult of human tasks, since in a given situation it is so easy either to apply the wrong principle or to rest in a statement of the right one, as if by magic it would apply itself. Physical grace, decorum, and the man-ners which follow upon the perception that in any society, including the academic one, there are rules and persons, not to speak of the improvement which can take place in any youth if he is surrounded by decent elders, may somehow increase with the college years. Again, however, there cannot be courses in such things.

It may be a travesty on the intention of those who call for moral education to speak as if they wanted courses, but to do so sharpens the point that a consciously cultivated character is an intolerable thing. "If it monopolize the man," says Emerson, "he is not yet sound, he does not yet know his wealth. He is in danger of becoming merely devout, and wearisome through the monotony of his thought." Character at its best, thought Woodrow Wilson, is a by-product of hard work well done; and he meant intellectual work. Which can remind us of the danger there may be in separating morals from mind. Thus separated, they can become so unimportant as to be contemptible or else so important as to be monstrous. Those communities are most vociferous about morality in which the least intellectual life goes on. So a college which advertises that it teaches character is sure to be one which knows how to do little else.

"The more we live by our intellect," said Tolstoy, "the less we understand the meaning of life." This could be true in some obscure and terrible sense for a man of his genius, but it has no meaning when parroted by commonplace persons who fear intellectual education as narrow, cold, or dry—their favorite adjectives, none of which is ever missing from the indictment. Those who thus attack it as "mere," implying some whole of which to be sure it would make a good part, usually want none of it at all, and show in their speech that they do not know what it is. At any rate, they should be asked whether they have undergone it, and if so whether they were able to observe that it had

nothing to do with emotion or love. It has everything to do
with them, though it respects them enough to desire that
they be rescued from cheap judgments of their worth. It
does not operate in a secluded place, "executing intellectual
minuets." It scarcely recognizes the distance which some
would put between moral education and itself. Itself is so
essential to education that unless all education is cold and
dry it cannot be. And it happens to be so bound up with
the moral virtues that if it does not exist, then they do not.
When it is zero, adding them to it still leaves zero. In spite
of the tenderhearted educators of our time who want to
protect youth from intellectual improvement, the parent
who sends his son to college continues to expect that the
alteration in him will be mental.

The conscious business of education is with the intellect.
The intellectual virtues, however, are many and difficult,
and some of them are native only to the farthest reaches of
self-education. These are the speculative virtues of understanding, science, and wisdom, with which the highest education does what it can. The arts of the intellect, as distinguished from its virtues, can be taught; and the traditional
duty of the college is to teach them. They are root faculties
without which there can be no further manhood. "What
but thought deepens life," asks Emerson, "and makes us
better than cow or cat?" There is no companion comparable to a mind that can be used; none more trustworthy
or agreeable. It can do things that nothing else can do. It
can explain how it is that of virtue in its essence there can
be no excess. It can ensure that our controversies are waged
on a level which the love of truth selects—"often a matter
of greater importance than the victory of either side." It
arms us against thugs who care only what we think, not

how. It assists us through the jungle of opinion where things only seem to exist, where beliefs only seem to be sufficient, and where conventions only seem to compel. It has its own hardships which it has learned how to endure; for it is difficult to think against desire; it is difficult to think at all, particularly for those who have not contracted the habit. It is the intellect that does these things for us, after we have trained it to concentrate upon those intelligible objects whose authority, once they are understood, is greater than that of any person. The work of education is to make them understood.

The danger in separating character from intellect and asking it to operate alone is that men will then be licensed to handle moral ideas as though they were not ideas. Without a capacity for abstraction we are blinded, like Plato's men emerging from their cave, by what we see. What we do not see is the nature of the thing we do. "Virtue is knowledge," said Socrates, who proved that the ignorant man cannot be courageous, for courage consists in knowing what is and what is not to be feared. Doubtless no one would deny that the world should be saved from ignorance. But a popular form of ignorance is the belief that life can be ordered by those who do not know what they are doing; fervor is enough. Our sincerity depends on our knowledge of what we are talking about. Morals cannot be better than thought. The soundest method of moral education is teaching how thought is done. "Let us endeavor then," says Pascal, "to think well; this is the principle of morality."

So it would appear that any radical disjunction of moral education and intellectual education is perilous. Character is both intellectual and moral. "Choice may be regarded either as an intelligence that desires or as a desire that reasons," says Aristotle, "and this combination makes the moving principle that is man." We do not want wisdom without goodness, but neither can we bear goodness without wisdom. Both take time to become perfect, and there is perhaps no moment in any life when they are evenly balanced; Emerson compared them with "the alternate periods of feeding and working in animals; each prepares and will be followed by the other." But they are mutually dependent, and at specific points, as for instance at the point where the moral virtue of desiring or willing to be taught must precede being taught, and where only courtesy decides that learning shall take place. It is moral virtue which makes a pupil studious rather than merely curious, to take one of Thomas Aquinas's memorable distinctions in this field; which makes the scholar brave enough for genuine inquiry; and which can save anyone from what Socrates called misology —the mistaken hatred of all ideas because some have turned out bad, the distrust of all reason because one has been deceived. It is moral character that gives us the strength to take the responsibility for our acts. And something even subtler lets us love the truth so that we may know it, gives us the power of delighting in whatever the mind has determined to be excellent. All of which can be summed up by saying that education has in prospect not so much the moral man as the good man; or, more simply, the man. "True morality," says Pascal, "makes light of morality." A safe and cheerful place to leave the subject, though it should be added that an answer has now been given to those who would ask the college to assume the functions of the family circle. Families will be better when education is better. When there is more of that, and when it is more liberal, better fathers and mothers will send their sons and daughters to school. The circle keeps on turning.

Liberal education is more than literary education, or moral education, or both. But how much more? It is time to say. And a convenient transition is through this theme of virtue which has been occupying our attention, possibly to a wearisome degree.

To possess virtue is a universal desire, even among those who would rather be thought evil than conventionally good. To them the conventions are not virtues, but they have their own conventions, and they do not think them evil. Thieves' honor is only one case of this. There is no human being who prefers to be known, at least by himself, as other than human. So all men are moral, for that is what to be moral means. It is the definitions that differ. From time to time, also, popular emphasis shifts; the cry is for some new set of virtues to replace the old one. Our young are belabored by editorials and orations to become at once warlike, or unwarlike; witty, or sobersided; docile, or independent. Interest in virtue is unending, though it is not invariably intelligent.

Liberal education tries to be intelligent about virtue; to find and keep the one definition of it that can weather change, that can outlive appearance; and to perfect a way by which it can be possessed. The last aim is practical, and therefore of great importance. Liberal education is nothing if not practical. It studies an art, or a system of arts, designed both by nature and by man to secure that human beings shall be precisely and permanently human.

The liberal quality may exist on any level of education, from the mother's knee to the most gorgeous cap and gown. But it is crucial at one point, which in America is the college. Late adolescence is the time of life when transformation is most natural. The common assumption is correct that more difference is made in a person by going to college than by anything else. Elementary education looks forward to this critical time, and the highest education builds upon whatever is then achieved. It is the moment when particular arts are mastered, or should be mastered: the arts which prepare the person for intellectual and moral virtues, the arts which will make those virtues possible in time. In so far as all education needs to be liberal in some sense, a liberal education can be set down as a complete education. But to do so is to obliterate a special meaning which tradition has lent the term.

"I call therefore a complete and generous education that which fits a man to perform justly, skillfully, and magnanimously all the offices both private and public of peace and war." Milton's famous sentence is a little broad for the present purpose, though for its own purpose it is flawless. It gives less attention than we must give to the notion of a capacity unfolded through four particular years, to the notion of an art which may convert, as Whitehead has put it, "the knowledge of a boy into the power of a man." The capacity in question has never been simple to define. It certainly includes the power to distinguish means from ends —confusion between which can so quickly generate fanatics and slaves. In itself, too, it is the power to multiply and explore choices, so that the world ceases to be a little place trimmed to the dimensions of one's private experience thus far. It can explain why George Washington, praising persons he knew, among them the officers in his command, reserved for a final compliment the epithet "liberal"; the word for him meant noble or large. And we shall do well to remember that for William James the opposite epithet was "literal"; the capacity is among other things a capacity in language, protecting its possessor against those failures of understanding which can arise when allegory is mistaken for fact, when symbol is seen as substance. But the list threatens to grow long. The main thing is that there are powers within the person which liberal education, and only liberal education, can free for use.

If the student asks why they should be freed, and for what use—to control what activity, to do what work with, to enable him to become what, and why—the reason could be that his society had not supplied him with a design for his own or any other life. The accusation that modern society so fails is in fact commonplace. But the student can do himself a good turn by disdaining to join the chorus. The powers under dispute are powers over nothing and nobody but himself. "The primary objects of desire are changes in one's self." The aim of liberal education is one's own excellence, the perfection of one's own intellectual character. Liberal education makes the person competent; not merely to know or do, but also, and indeed chiefly, to be. A student to whom this can mean nothing would learn little from any society. The only thing that can teach him its meaning is liberal education—the argument once more is circular. The task of liberal education is to make itself loved so that the end it seeks, excellence, may in turn be loved.

The prime occupation of liberal education is with the skills of being. There are those who promise lesser skills in its name. It has been called a focus for the mind, which then becomes a searchlight ready to be turned on any field of vision. Huxley, pursuing the mechanical figure to its end, said that the liberal intellect was a steam engine "with all its parts of equal strength, and in smooth working order, ready to be turned to any kind of work." The image is depressing, not merely because it is mechanical but because it refers to the future: education is something to be intellectually cashed in. Liberal education is now.

If the student wonders whether his own being is end enough, that is because he does not yet know the difference between himself as individual and as person. "Know thyself" was an oracle addressed to the individual, charging him to become a person; to know, as a matter of fact, almost everything other than himself, to know the world for what it is, for what it "honestly and deeply means," and above all to substitute for the inquiry "What do I think?" the inquiry "What can be thought?" The emphasis is not upon his reason but upon reason; not upon himself but upon his kind. Obeying the oracle, he endeavors to rear within himself that third man who is present when two men speak, and who is happy when they understand each other.

It is not an easy end, and it takes courage to desire it—courage here as always consisting in the knowledge of what is and what is not to be feared. What is not to be feared is possible unsuccess in livelihood or fame. What is to be feared is deadness, now or later. But the very means are arduous, and they may be painful. Liberal education has been called a surgery of the soul, which suggests that the result is more agreeable than the operation. The knife employed is sharper than flattery, and it cuts deeper than opinion's skin. Liberal education has also been called a tempering process—in both senses, surely, of a term which can mean either to toughen or to make less tough. The temperate man is the tempered man, both as steel and as the wind

are tempered, for stern work and the shorn lamb. The educated person is gentle, but he is at the same time a tough
spirit. He is the least surprised among those who find life
hard, for that is what he has been taught it will be. Gentle
enough to love justice, he is firm enough to insist that it be
more than justice for himself. Life for him is hard because
he must always think about it, and thinking is hard; and it
is exciting because it bristles with decisions which fill his
days with crisis and color them with possible tragedy. He
lives with ideas, but for him they are not neutral food. He
resists them at first in the way that all men do; but once
they have forced an entrance, he knows how to play the
muscles of his mind upon them, and how to eject again the
insipid or the vile.

He must be prepared, too, for resistance in the world to
what he represents. The thinking man is not readily popular. Disinterested criticism is disturbing, for it is criticism
which never ceases, and it is stubborn with real questions
to which there may be no quick answers. Matthew Arnold's
description of the great man of culture as one who divests
knowledge of all that is "harsh, uncouth, difficult, abstract"
is less than the truth. The liberally educated person will
be as difficult as the subject he discusses—no more so, but
certainly no less—and he will be harsh if he has to. William
James was appalled by the "atrocious harmlessness" of the
thought that went on at Lake Chautauqua. The poorest
compliment we could pay liberal education would be to
say that it produced activity like that. It is to be recommended, and it may be loved, but there will always be some
who find it harmful to their peace. It is a gift. It is also a
hazard.

Our talk of it, however, has been general long enough.

We have praised it and made claims for it, but it has not been shown at work. The reality rather than the name is what we seek. The content of liberal education is never indeterminate. Tools are to be mastered; things are to be learned. The liberal education in America which now is doubted by so many was not altogether worth saving. Such of it as survives will be that part which, like truth, is never mocked. It is the part capable of demonstrating that bad thinking brings bad consequences, now or at any time. "Nature," prophesies Albert Jay Nock, "takes her own time, sometimes a long time, about exacting her penalty, and often gets at it by strange, unexpected, and roundabout ways; but exact it in the end she always does, and to the last penny. . . . A society which takes no account of the educable person, makes no place for him, does nothing for him, is taking a considerable risk; so considerable that in the whole course of human experience, as far as our records go, no society ever yet has taken it without coming to great disaster." The notion of Nock is that only a few are educable, whereas the thesis of this book is that many are, and indeed all men. But numbers do not matter now. The liberal education to be saved for us at last is a substance of which we have had the shadow. This almost means that it must be created, or at any rate revived from an older time when it was real. Revival would mean the rediscovery of the arts and the knowledge necessary to its life at any time.

V

The Liberal Arts

Tᴴᴇ ᴡᴏʀᴅ "liberal" before the word "education" has a long history, and in that history it has a meaning. Both the history and the meaning are little known today, with the result that liberal in many minds suggests only certain studies which lie outside the fields of exact knowledge—or perhaps it would be better to say, in view of the vagueness attributed to them even by those who grant them "cultural" grace, uncertain studies. In the preceding chapter it was said that they were supposed by some to be the Greek and Roman classics, "English," and "the humanities." The list could have been longer; here we can add a seasoning of history and a dash of philosophy on its more harmless, that is to say its descriptive, side, where it will be discovered making no claims for itself as knowledge, exact or otherwise.

The right reference in the word "liberal" is to a family of arts which also have their history and their meaning. But again there is the meagerest general acquaintance even with the names of these arts, and there is little curiosity as to

their function, so that "colleges of the liberal arts" are seldom challenged to defend or explain such a title; and out
of the thousands who annually become "masters" of the
same arts, proceeding thence to teach under their sign, only
a handful ever know what they have been dubbed masters
of. They are usually more than willing to be let pass as
persons with no special equipment who hope to finish the
intellectual journey in that comfort which comes from knowing that examinations are over. If the word "arts" in this
connection means anything to the public, it means, vaguely,
the fine arts including literature, perhaps along with enough
education in general subjects to quiet the question which
may be asked of a minority later on: Of what philosophy
have they become doctors? Most such doctors trust that they
will never have to think up an answer.

The liberal arts, whether or not the fact is known, are
specific arts, clearly distinguished from other arts and performing necessary human functions. These functions are
performed even by those who do not know their names, provided they live at all, for such functions are a condition of
life. But they are performed better, and with a happier result of understanding, when we study their rules. Education
will be better when there is more curiosity about the arts
of which it is still possible to be declared master.

The liberal arts are but a few of the innumerable arts
which anyone possesses or may possess. The average man
seems not to know that he is an artist with every step he
takes, for walking is an art; with every door he opens, for
knobs and keys are the instruments of an art; with every
mouthful he swallows, for eating is an art; with every glance
at his watch, for reading the position of two radii is an art;
with every word he speaks, for language is an art. He had

to learn them all, as in the capacity of parent he will have to teach them all; and there are countless others which by a strange oversight we neglect to pride ourselves in. The boy on the farm is possessed of a hundred arts—having to do with traces, bolts, maple sugar, seed wheat, carburetors, crankshafts, and cams—which he is too modest to put forward as a claim to distinction, though in possessing them he is distinguished from millions of individuals who live at the same time in the same world.

He, or any other person uninitiated in the terms of his dexterity, is likely to suppose that the only arts are those of the painter, the poet, the architect, the sculptor, and the musician. But those are the fine arts, whereas his are the useful arts. Both classes are essential to life, and for the moment we need not inquire whether one class is more important than the other, or more admirable. The arts classify themselves with fair ease, and it is edifying to remember the traditional names of the classes. It is an old story, for instance, that Nature has her arts; water knows how to spread in circles when a pebble strikes a pond, thunder knows how to travel among the clouds, and the body which we know how to feed knows how to digest.

If the natural arts be set aside as independent of man's control—though this would be misleading, for all of his arts co-operate with them and proceed from them—the human arts that remain fall into the three great classes of useful, liberal, and fine. The liberal arts are always, and properly, left in a middle position between those with which we manipulate objects and those with which we create them— or, if man cannot in reality create, with which we render individual things, such as a hero in story or a form in painting, more luminous than they were. The liberal arts are the specifically intellectual arts, and therefore are keys to all of man's operations as man. They are basic to the life he lives in so far as it is unique; for his intellect may have no counterpart elsewhere. Their activity is assumed in the useful and the fine arts, but it is an activity which can perfect itself, and which does so through a discipline of the intellect aiming to make it aware of its powers. In the present context its powers amount to a skill in reading words and things; in contemplating the special materials of human experience, and in handling them so that they assist in the recognition and the expression of truth. They are central to education, for they command the mind at the point where it does any work it has to do. Their two most familiar names are language and mathematics.

So far we have considered the educated person entirely as a product. The process of which he is a product is the process of mastering the liberal arts; or, if a more modest term be preferred, of acquiring them. No one is educated who has not done this. But most current talk about education is content with optimistic guesses that any given student, no matter what his training has been, and no matter how little precision has characterized it, will somehow come out of it with the right feelings and ideas, an excellent fellow who has absorbed his heritage. A portion of his heritage is, of course, inescapable, but the bulk of it is not available to one who is undisciplined in discourse. Scarcely an educator fails to boast of the skills his students carry away with them. Few educators, however, could guarantee that these skills are principal or liberal, and that the method by which they were acquired is one which they themselves have fashioned in line with the best that has been thought and known.

THE LIBERAL ARTS

The liberal arts are the maturing rituals of our civilized tribe. The ethnologist discusses similar rituals in the case of peoples whom we do not dignify with the epithet, and nobody doubts that in doing so he tells us much about those peoples. We hear less about the rites by which we are expected to initiate ourselves into the race of intellectual man. This is partly because we think that being civilized means we are beyond ritual, but it is partly an accident of history: we have forgotten the gestures and the music.

There is a well-known legend about the citizen who wakes up at forty to find himself going through a routine the meaning of which he has never known, and the value of which he now may doubt. His days repeat themselves, and he cannot find a theme among the more or less dead sounds they make when they strike in time. The reason could be that he had missed the heart of the human doctrine, which deals with repetition, routine, and refrain. Life is monotonous. The arts, and especially the liberal arts, know what to make of the fact: how much to accept it and dignify it with duties, how much to defy it or correct it with pleasure, pretense, play, and speculation. The heathen of forty is only one case in point. When the liberal arts fail to do their work, civilization has become a disease. When they are dismissed as a luxury, practical affairs suffer the consequence. They are the most practical possession men have, and they proceed by method, not by knack. Education is not had at random, though we have been acting as if that were the case.

We glibly list the skills and the knowledges that mark an educated man without inquiring whether there is a necessary relation between the columns of terms. The truth is that habits of skill are prerequisite to learning, and habits

[75]

of learning are prerequisite to skill. In the useful arts this is easier to see: we must learn to do so that we shall be able to make, but in making we learn how to do. Yet it is almost as plain in the liberal arts, where the art of knowing both precedes recognition and is a form of recognition. The liberal arts are a preparation for the intellectual virtues, and at the same time they are practiced well only by those who have intellectual virtue. There is the circle again from which no serious discussion of education—or of any other practical thing—escapes.

The liberal arts are an education in the human language, which should be as universal among men as the human form, and yet is not. St. Augustine paid his education the compliment of saying that as a result of it he could read anything that was written, understand anything he heard said, and say anything he thought. This is perhaps as much praise as education could desire. It is rarely deserved, and the reason is that we are not taught the complexities of the human language. Man means both more and less than he says; there is no such thing as a statement that exactly matches its maker's thought. We talk either nonsense or in figures, and paradox is our grammar. The uneducated person either ignores the paradoxes or is infuriated by them; or at best is puzzled. Many a familiar statement, if it is familiar enough, passes as simple. "Man is a rational animal." Is he? He is, but the sentence has been argued for centuries; and the mere fact that it does not die out as a commonplace is proof of its bold, strange, and always original power, as if it spoke a double language; which it does. This is not to say that men speak only to fool one another. That can be done, but when they are most sincere they share their allegories. The liberal arts familiarize us with the standard allegories, and prepare us to cope with those of the poets, the mathematicians, the scientists, and the metaphysicians which are rarer. The human language, once it is admitted to be complex, reveals itself as cogent. But bad education does not assist the revelation; it leaves us, on the contrary, chronically misunderstanding our enemies and friends.

The natural arts are not to be forgotten. The artist of nature is the one whom human artists imitate. This is most frequently seen in the doctor who as an artist in medicine tries to discover the principles of health which the artist of the body practices—sometimes imperfectly—and then the doctor, we say, helps nature to achieve its end. But the assistance takes the form of imitation, as in poetry a human artist not so much invents as uses what he knows when he tells a story; he assists the logic and ethics of human events to express themselves. The formula is less familiar to those who speak of the liberal arts without knowing what they are. They are physicians too, imitating and assisting the natural process of learning. For man learns a great deal without teachers at all; teachers did not originate the faculty or process. They only study how learning takes place, and help it to do so economically, swiftly, and richly; endeavoring always to save the individual to whom the thing is happening those long delays—of millenniums, or even of geologic ages—which he would suffer if he had not the past of his race to help him. Not that nature, either here or in the medicine of the body, is easy to know. Nature has its own double talk and its delight in concealment. Nature is the first thing that is, but the last thing we know. All the cultivation of which we are capable will barely make us natural enough. A paradox? But it is what the man means who says he is not educated. His mind is not his second nature, at home both in him and in the world.

The liberal arts make us expert in the species of things and in their quantities—what kind? and how much? Their aim is exactness, even to the point which Aristotle had in mind when he said it was the mark of an educated intellect "to seek only so much exactness in each type of inquiry as may be allowed by the nature of the subject matter." He meant, presumably, the right kind of exactness in any given case. The wrong kind produces the wrong results, if any at all. A counting of the syllables in Shakespeare's lines may be numerically exact, but it tells us nothing of Shakespeare's "numbers"—that is, his rhythm—let alone his feeling or his fancy. The lover can add up his mistress's charms and still fail to convince us that she is divine. The truant boy can be so exhaustive in his excuses that we know he is lying, as the hostess knows by our five engagements that we do not want to accept her invitation. There is no such thing as too much exactness; man wants as much as he can get.

Too much of one thing means that another thing has put in its appearance; the line that has been crossed is the line of kind, not of degree. The liberal artist is trained to walk such fences. Too much kindness is impossible; it is condescension that has come, or a gluttony for doing good. Too much clarity is unthinkable; it is the imagination that has disappeared, under pressure from logic which has forgotten its aim. There is no weaker statement than this: Freedom is good up to a certain point, but after that it is bad. There is no satisfaction like that of learning the name of the thing different from freedom which then exists; and only intellect can supply the name. So with the line which divides theory from practice, or that other one which is the boundary between particulars and universals. Or the network of lines which expose the anatomy of a crisis. The need in a crisis is for skill in differentiation between alternatives.

The liberal arts are the liberating arts. They involve memory, calculation, manipulation, and measurement, and call for dexterity of both mind and hand. Without these powers no mind is free to be what it desires. The mind itself desires to be free—from the animal within, from the enigma without. It most of all desires to be free of the individual who was born possessing it. We can use no mind except our own, but the more we use it, and the better, the closer it is in its resemblance to whatever other minds have been used well. Our mind desires to be the human mind.

"All men," says Comenius, "fleeing outward from themselves, seek in the world and its things wherewith to calm and quiet their minds. . . . The world is our school." It is not merely that the mind must order itself; it must order as well as it can the world and its multitude of things. The liberal arts are more than cosmetic, beautifying their possessor with grace. When they are only that, if indeed they can be only that, they are a nuisance and a danger. Their view is outward, to the things of the world in their kinds and quantities; for it is when these kinds and quantities are dark to us that the world makes us slaves. We can conquer it only by understanding, which in the case of the liberal arts means naming and measuring. The subject matter of the liberal arts is life.

They are exacting arts, and it will be difficult for an age which has lost contact with them to restore the sense that they are necessary. Nevertheless this must be done if we are to keep faith in the importance of liberal education, and if we are to know what we are talking about when we state that faith. The sign that the liberal arts are present in a discussion is its quality, in whatever degree, of light and precision. Precision, if not abundant light, now marks one area of education only, the area known as science. The light there would be richer if it were not confined like a candle in the dark, yet it is a light, and the world looks there most confidently for something it can respect. The task for education is to spread this light, to make itself liberal everywhere, to give its essential arts work to do in every room of the house. Only then will the house become a civilized habitation, with light and warmth uniformly distributed. Until such a moment arrives, the places where art thrives are places of black art, or art turned esoteric, rather than of that white kind which Prospero on his enchanted isle practiced in competition with a whole world grown competent in savagery. The art of Prospero was magic, and it was most potent. But his name for it was "liberal." And if he buried it deeper than did ever plummet sound, there is no reason why it should not be dug up again. The difference between liberal education and any other kind is still magical, for the powers it releases are not to be matched elsewhere.

If they are especially difficult to release, the best explanation is the old one: we are mixed creatures. The tiger's powers are visible and available. The archangel's are available but invisible. Man, who is neither pure body nor pure mind, carries his capacities in a part of him that is hard to get at; and even in the noblest person they may never be crystal-clear. But he has arts with which to elicit them. "The symbols of language and mathematics are the only symbols that are realized in human knowledge," says Scott Buchanan. "They are our mother tongue. It is for this reason that the liberal arts hold the central position in traditional education, and that our success in them is the measure of our success in all other arts."

But what are the liberal arts by name? Tradition, grounded in more than two millenniums of intellectual history, calls them grammar, rhetoric, and logic; arithmetic, music, geometry, and astronomy. As names these may be disappointing; some may sound narrow, others remote. And the objection might be offered that it is not the names that matter so much as the essential operations, wherefore the discussion should get ahead to the operations. Even then, however, the operations would have to be named if they were to be kept clear of one another, and their natures understood. And no new names have been found. So the old ones, numbering seven, must be saved until such time as their meaning can be transferred without loss to another set.

The liberal arts are seven, but a division occurs between the first three, which Latin Europe called the trivium, and the last four, which it called the quadrivium. "I doubt," said Huxley, "if the curriculum of any modern university shows so clear and generous a comprehension of what is meant by culture as this old trivium and quadrivium does." There is a great advantage in names. We have reduced seven to two: the trivium is literature and the quadrivium is mathematics. But in doing so we have lost more than the numerical difference of five. Within each division we have suppressed distinctions, and by forgetting that the single name for them all is "the seven liberal arts" we have failed to keep in mind their unity of purpose, with the result that it has become possible to suppose that some are more liberal than others, or indeed that the others are not liberal at all. The common view today, for instance, is of literature as

[81]

being more liberal than mathematics and science. But this is a double error. Not only does the quadrivium belong to the whole enterprise as a partner; in contemporary practice it is actually mathematics and science that preserve in highest degree the precision which all of the seven arts once conspired to promote. The point is that they did conspire, as seven partners no less than as two. Each depended upon the rest; they penetrated one another, letting light in everywhere.

The arts of the trivium can be rechristened as reading, writing, and thinking; this in fact has been done, and there is a certain initial advantage in terms which sound less academic than their ancestors. The disadvantage is that the new terms emphasize words at the expense of things, leaving an impression more literary than intellectual. Man may be unable to know things in themselves, but when his language is most alive its words refer to things as well as to themselves. When reading, writing, and thinking proceed on both levels, protecting words against the temptation of self-love, the result is the one desired. The levels are more clearly specified, however, by the terms grammar, rhetoric, and logic, which live on both of them: grammar as "the operation of particular things in discourse," rhetoric as "the signifying of some particular things through other particular things," and logic as "the relation of all things to universals." To think thus is better than to think of grammar as nothing but parts of speech, rhetoric as nothing but tricks of the speaking trade, and logic as nothing but verbal conclusions. Those are important, and they are not studied enough. But it is better to view the three arts as prepared to read a text of objects no less than a page of letters—to read them, to expand their meaning, and to interpret them. That is what science has been described as doing in its three stages of observation, experimentation, and prediction; and the doctor as doing in diagnosis, prognosis, and therapy.

All human work has its grammar, rhetoric, and logic; every man practices them his life long. He practices them better when he knows that he is doing so and can name the processes; when he knows that he is incessantly an artist, either of the trivium, when he distinguishes the kinds of things, or of the quadrivium, when he handles their quantities. We cling to the elementary prescription of reading, writing, and arithmetic; whenever there seems to be a danger of our forgetting what children should be taught, we thus remember and reform. Higher education might cling with equal tenacity to the seven liberal arts.

Their history has not been smooth or even. At no time have they flourished in an absolutely right relation. If their relation was more or less perfect at some stage of Greek education when a marriage occurred between language and mathematics, it lost symmetry at Rome, where rhetoric dominated everything and grammar was the study of literature alone. The early Christians resisted the liberal arts as secular, but their successors saw them as an intellectual support for any advance religion would make, and by the fourth century they were established again; St. Augustine left treatises on six of them, and the following centuries were busy exploring their connections. Seven hundred years after St. Augustine, Hugo of Saint-Victor decided that the trivium yields knowledge of words and the quadrivium yields knowledge of things—perhaps an unfortunate separation. Grammar for Hugo deals with expression, rhetoric with meaning, and logic with both. With respect to the form of things, arithmetic studies their number, music their proportion, geometry their dimension, and astronomy their motion; with respect to the nature or internal quality of things, the whole quadrivium proceeds under the name physics. The medieval universities, however, were not constant or uniform in their distribution of the emphasis; though nothing occurred in their thinking to match the split that came in the seventeenth century, when the new science developed the quadrivium as an exclusive discipline, only purloining logic from the trivium because it was indispensable; and when the old literary learning countered with an equally exclusive discipline in the trivium. It was then that language (or literature) and mathematics (or science) became the enemies they still are.

They wage unnecessary war in which each side loses much that it originally possessed. The study of literature, as has already been suggested, is no longer a logical study, and latterly it has abandoned rhetoric to advertising and propaganda. It is left with nothing but grammar—which, because it works in isolation, knows its terms but one at a time, and naïvely. The literature of Europe and America grows steadily more childish. So science, working in a similar vacuum, though working well, threatens to confine itself to facts, and therefore to the one art of observation, which again is grammar. All of the seven arts have sunk, in the worst view that can be taken of them, to "grammars without rules." Such a view would explain the prevailing ignorance as to what any given study is for, and as to the kind or degree of freedom it is capable of bestowing upon him who pursues it. Freedom of what, for what? Those questions in turn become meaningless, and are seldom asked. That is why the educator knows little more than the student concerning the relative worth of subjects, and so, at any rate until recently, has been content to let the student decide among them.

The educator by tradition is a liberal artist who knows his seven disciplines and imposes them upon the pupil who comes to him. Tradition licenses him to be lopsided, to favor this order or that. But there are seven items which he orders, and he knows their names. Without their names the contemporary teacher is either a pretender or a specialist. He is usually the latter, and as such he may be valuable. But his value would be increased if as a scientist he could manage hypotheses as expertly as he manages facts, or if as a humanist he remembered that words refer to things as well as to themselves, and that being has its own imagination, life its own logic. The hope for education lies in the chance that it can recover its faith in the liberal arts. There is nothing sacred in their number, or perhaps in their nomenclature. The operations are the thing. But the operations suffered when the names disappeared. Both may be necessary again.

THE LEVELS OF EDUCATION

No one escapes education. It comes with pleasure, work, and disappointment, through friends and lovers, in laws and customs, religion and popular art, posters and proverbs; and it lurks behind every name we hear publicly celebrated, for that this man should be a hero tells us more sometimes than all the other oracles together.

But such education is unconscious and informal. The education of which everyone is aware proceeds by definite stages; the student, growing older, advances to new levels of difficulty for which we have not only terms but institutions. It is important to ask how many levels are natural and therefore necessary; what should happen on each; and how the relations between them are to be considered. A further question, still more relevant to this book, has to do with the means for making all of them more liberal. The word may be read freely, as meaning good, proper, or complete; or it can suggest the limited function so far assigned to the arts called liberal. In the latter case the discussion would be of the means whereby education on all levels could better assist those arts in performing their function in the right way at the right time. This might involve a policy on the lower levels of not anticipating their activity misguidedly or too soon, and on the highest level of supporting their effort by a respectful attempt to capitalize their result. Specifically in America the discussion would be about education before and after college; the search would be for a formula to minimize ignorance or confusion concerning the kinds of education.

The responsible educator wants to know all he can about the steps the mind takes as it grows. There must be a natural order of learning. As the eye delights to look, Comenius tells us, so the mind thirsts for objects, and is indefatigible in absorbing them provided they are presented "one after the other, and in the proper order." It is the vision of such an order that teases every philosopher of education, sometimes to become profound, sometimes to be absurd. The proper one may not be found till doomsday; but no educator is true to his trust who does not try to find it.

It is doubtless an order among degrees, not kinds. Education at its heart is all one kind. "The truly important order," says Whitehead, "is the order of quality." There never are new subjects, but the old ones rise to new levels of depth or difficulty; the student is ever pursuing the same truth on different landings. It will never be wholly known, just as the secret of how to teach it will never be any man's exclusive possession. When education means anything fundamental, however, it refers to an orderly ascent of the stairs.

The consensus, ancient and modern, seems to be that there are three natural or necessary levels: elementary, liberal, and professional. These can be variously stated, and of course they are. The first can be called preparatory, the second intellectual, and the third practical—if practical is understood as meaning the full use in maturity of the mind that has been made free for employment. The first can be said to have in view the improvement of the creature through a wise exercise of his senses, his memory, and his imagination; the second can be described as a discipline in abstraction, an introduction to ideas; and the third can be set down as philosophy at work. It may or may not be easy to recognize behind all this the American grammar school, high school, college, and university. But there they are, and the question is how they shall adjust themselves to the immemorial triple division of low, middle, and high, or young, maturing, and mature.

Plato's scheme began with gymnastic, music, and letters; went on to the abstractions of the quadrivium; and ripened in metaphysics. Comenius, who would have education commence in infancy, at home, and be systematic there, projected three institutions to follow: the vernacular school, occupied with the three R's, morality, and the mechanical arts; the Latin school, devoted to the liberal arts; and the university, where the sciences were to be pursued. Whitehead has named three stages to which these institutions, or their equivalents, conform. They are the stages of "romance, precision, and generalization." And Maritain has suggested three corresponding forms of truth: as beauty, as reason, and as knowledge. But those are details of interpretation, not a further ordering of the levels.

It remains to say that the consensus keeps two other points clearly in view. Elementary education is for a time before the intellect is ready to do its work. And the order with respect to liberal and advanced studies is from the arts to the sciences, from the unchanging to the changing, from the permanent studies, as William Whewell has named them, to the progressive studies. Liberal education is an education in what all men must know; university education deals with what some men may know, building beyond this base. It is perhaps obvious that liberal education, holding the middle position, depends upon elementary education to prepare its students rightly, and upon university education to honor the breach between the permanent and the progressive—which means more simply to leave the college free.

Elementary education deserves a special glance because the liberal educator is chronically dissatisfied with the condition in which it sends him his students, and because for any observer it has its own fascinations. No feat is more amazing than the feat of the child in learning how to read, write, figure, and think. We do not know how the small savage thus becomes a son of truth. We only know that he does it, and that certain circumstances help him to do it happily and well. It is important that he should be happy while he does it, or—this puts it better—that doing it should make him happy. When he goes on to college ill-prepared, the explanation may be that his school has mishandled him:

expected too little from him, or too much of the wrong thing. The right animal may have been put through the wrong paces.

"Don't let them eat their seed corn," said Emerson, meaning that students cannot afford to "be young men before they have finished their boyhood." Rousseau, who could be both foolish and wise, was not foolish when he wrote that "childhood is the sleep of reason." Whatever we do for the child, he is doing one very important thing by himself: he is growing up. This is not to say that he lacks reason, but to suggest that reason in him had better not be hurried; for it prefers to lie in wait for its proper moment, and until then will often be stubborn and ashamed if its limitations are exposed, or retreat into deeper places than will be good for it later on. It desires cultivation even now, but simply and with ample attention to the senses, which are the suit it wears.

The child knows when he is being bullied by the reason of his elders. It is something with which he cannot cope, although he understands that it is being used to force him into unnatural roles. He is given the morning's news, for instance, and asked what he would do if he were Winston Churchill; or he is elected a member of some little imitation league, some mock economic conference, and watched to see whether he will behave like the man he of course is not. For the teacher thus to assume in pupils experience which nothing could have given them is a crime against the very reason that is growing in them but wishes now to be left intact. The elementary pupil, quite as much as the liberal student, wants to do what he can do; and this is not to advance the world's knowledge. It is to catch up with as much of it as can be understood. The child, even more than the young man, is set for permanent studies. His job is not to understand whatever world may flash by at the moment; it is to get himself ready for any human world at all.

Rousseau would have kept his pupil a savage until fifteen. That was absurd, for the child does not wish to be a savage. His human powers are to be cultivated to their limit. But this limit should be known. The exercise of his reason should be not so much in terms of its process as in terms of its feeding; what it will need later, and cannot have got otherwise, should now be given it as richly and delightfully as possible. It is the materials for reason that elementary education can supply. The child can and should be taught to notice, to remember, and to make. His observation, his memory, and his imagination are to be trained. There is no better time to do so than now. Later may be too late.

The child exists gladly. He has a natural disposition to know; he prefers knowing the truth; he admires justice; he has his heroes; and he approves of work when it is well done. It is not the ideal child who is being described, it is any child with whose nature nothing has interfered. He is expected to be happy, and generally is blamed if he is not. But what makes him most unhappy is an education which takes the wrong view of his desire to be a man. If he dreams of greatness, he knows he is not great yet. He is willing that all of his activity should prepare him for the moment when he shall be grown, but he wants this preparation to strike a sane balance between the solemn and the playful. All education is not for him; he is not its end; yet he would prefer this beginning stage, while it keeps the end in view, to respect him as a creature of intrinsic importance, desirous of enjoying what is about to be learned. The full prescription is never met. No parent or teacher has ever deserved to be complacent as he contemplated the result of his labors. But this does not mean that we should be less wise than we can.

The three R's rightly recognize and state the studies which are proper in elementary education because they require no special knowledge or experience for their comprehension. Language, literature, mathematics, and certain of the sciences are adaptable to this level. To adapt them, however, does not mean to make them easy through adult textbooks which have been whittled down. Textbooks are pernicious at any stage of education if they are given more to do than teach the teacher what some greater master of the subject knows. In themselves they are toneless teachers, without the advantage of presence or voice; they are a technical help of which the student should be unaware. When they are in effect the only teacher he has, he tends to become "an instructed, bewildered intellectual dwarf." He would rather hear, see, and handle, for then he will remember and imagine.

The child is properly interested in the useful arts, and is happy if he can practice them as a kind of poetry. If he is permitted to discover their principles as he works, he will already have made contact with general ideas; and it will be still better if the principles he discovers are important. This will be the case if the skills he is encouraged to seek are classic skills, somewhat as the games of children are classic—old, and dignified with ritual. Poetry as such will then be no foreigner to his imagination, and he will know when it is most real, he will have begun to be a critic; especially if all that he does is done in an order "calculated to stimulate his imagination and emotions, and directed so as to become disciplines." Reading, writing, and arithmetic are best learned in the setting of art—of use and play. Their theoretical part can be made thus to yield its meaning directly, without the intervention of misleading terms. If the word "play" worries anyone, he should remember that children are never so serious as when they are making things up.

The foregoing paragraphs might appear to be a description of what today is called progressive education. Within limits it is, for progressive education has hold of a good tradition; it is not physically brutal, and it makes no monstrous claims on the child's reason. Also, it assumes that the child is to be happy while he learns. So far there is nothing in it newer than Plato, just as there is nothing in it with which a sensible and humane adult could disagree.

Progressive education, however, misses being perfect elementary education when it ignores two things: the deep resemblances between human beings, calling for a fixed program of learning which no child may evade, and the importance of the human past.

"By dint of insisting that in order to teach John mathematics it is more important to know John than to know mathematics—which is true enough in one sense—the teacher will so perfectly succeed in knowing John that John will never succeed in knowing mathematics." This sentence of Maritain's is more than witty, it points to the primacy of the thing to be learned; and it assumes that John is like any other boy in needing to be taught. He does not need to exist, for he exists already; but his very existence presupposes a readiness to know what the mind can know at this stage. It is his mind that is to be educated, and it must be assumed that his mind is human. It may have special powers and graces, and one hopes it has. They will make themselves known, however, only when the regular business has been done. The teacher's business is regular. It is the only way in the long run to ripen those individual differences which some progressive educators prefer to pick and leave in the raw.

Freedom in a child is like freedom in any human being; discipline is wanted to bring it out. There is no beaten track of instinct down which the child knows without teaching how to run. He hesitates, is undetermined, and is suggestible. There are suggestions which he cannot and will not take, and this is one sign of his freedom; but there are others for which he will be grateful, and these will grow into another sign of his freedom. The teacher who withholds his authority when it is desired is like the friend who will never give advice; he is no true teacher. If he says in excuse that tyranny destroys individuals, he has forgotten that persons starve without guidance, and love those who lead them well. An error in direction could scarcely be worse than refusal to direct. Most progressive education is libeled when it is accused of refusing to lead—to perform, that is, "the duty of the adult to the freedom of the youth." When it does so refuse, there seems to be no reason why it should be known as education at all. The child does not want to be cheap, but left to his own devices he may miss what is most dear. He should and will forgive no teacher who thus abandons him.

The progressive educator could profit by learning the traditional language of his art. When he is ignorant of it he has no armor against the lingo of his contemporaries, many of whom seem to believe that education began yesterday, along with human life. The world does change, but not to know exactly what this means is to underrate the forces which have been in the past so that the present could be. Too many progressive educators worship this world. It may be bad enough to worship the world, but this world alone is less than the child deserves to be given. And the truth is that there is no such thing. There is a temporal depth behind every living form, an immense antiquity in which most of its meaning resides. The child loves knowing that his environment has more than spatial dimension. The context of his life is not confined to the contemporary, and even though this is never to be the explicit burden of the teaching he gets—for he is no antiquarian—it can remain like an aroma of authority over everything he hears. The perhaps mythical child who is ordered to do what he pleases knows that if nothing else his family has conditioned his choice. He might know that his family has been conditioned by thousands of generations before it, and that there is such a thing as common wisdom the source of which even scholars do not pretend to trace. When Gargantua commanded that the words "Do what thou wilt" be posted over the doorway at the abbey of Thélème, he understood that those who would read them were already possessed, happily or not, with principles of order. They are in us whether we like it or no. And education is the thing that tells us whether they are good. It should not suppress the probability that they are as hoary as the human race.

Elementary education can do nothing better for a child than store his memory with things deserving to be there. He will be grateful for them when he grows up, even if he kicks now. They should be good things; indeed, they should be the best things, and all children should possess them. Some of the problems which society is said to face in the future might already be on their way to a solution if all persons then were certain to have common sentiments, and the sentiments were sound. Educational research in the fields of janitor service and reaction-counting might switch to the question of what children ought to remember. Education can afford to hold conferences about this for a hundred years; about this, and about the content of teaching on every higher level; for education will be saved only when it is agreed that men must know the same things—which does not mean that they will believe the same things. It means rather that they will be protected, in the only way education can bring this about, against mass judgments at the eleventh hour.

Memory is the mother of imagination, reason, and skill. "We estimate a man by how much he remembers," says Emerson. "We like signs of richness in an individual, and most of all we like a great memory. Memory performs the impossible for man; holds together past and present, gives continuity and dignity to human life. This is the companion, this the tutor, the poet, the library, with which you travel. Any piece of knowledge I acquire today has a value at this moment exactly proportioned to my skill to deal with it. Tomorrow, when I know more, I recall that piece of knowledge and use it better." It might seem that Emerson had said everything on the subject, but he added: "The reason of the short memory is shallow thought." If he had taken one more breath and said, "The reason for shallow thought is a short memory," he would have exhausted his topic.

There should be no school in which the young mind fails to receive, like seeds destined to germinate in later years, a full sowing of sentences great men have spoken—poems or parts of poems, and passages of prose—along with pieces of powerful music, glimpses of powerful painting, classical formulas in mathematics, chemistry, and physics, and the patterns of certain instruments without which science is helpless. We take it for granted that the multiplication tables must be learned, but these other things are no less necessary to the mind. Passages of verse or prose come back to us in middle age with interest which there are no tables to compute; if they were put there to stay, they may modify every thought and action when thought and action count. A medical diagnostician of our day attributes many of his insights to the lines of poetry his father once made him learn; their influence is indirect, but all the more potent for that reason. And this influence is more than something he uses in his trade. The good in such cases is general. So likewise with those items of memory which are more important still: early images of noble men—Socrates, for a single example. There is no later substitute for these.

"Modern imagination," says Scott Buchanan, "is notoriously weak and spastic"; and his explanation is our failure in schools to train the memory so that it can hold on to good things. But the good things have to be put there first, no matter with what effort. The effort at best is great, though imagination in the teacher can make it agreeable. This is true not only for words but for operations—of the reason in mathematics, where Locke has eloquently shown how indispensable memory is to understanding, and of the hands in shop or studio, where education also goes on.

Education is of the hand as well as of the head and heart. Some of our gray matter seems to be in the fingers, which had better be familiar with their hidden wisdom. Mere readers and talkers are never subtle enough. "The second-handedness of the learned world," says Whitehead, "is the secret of its mediocrity." There is in men a "deep natural instinct to translate thought into manual skill, and manual activity into thought." The child comprehends nothing which he is forbidden to touch. Manually incompetent persons are to that extent intellectually incompetent persons; they are imperfect liberal artists for whom the serenity and the precision of the workshop remain mythical joys. Knowing includes knowing how to do, whether in poetry or in mechanics, whether with levers or with laws; and a time promises to come when the distinction between brain and hand is divested of its present snobbery. So the school has a manual task, which should be more than pottering with sticks and wheels. Here again the memory is waiting to be filled with fair and permanent things: the crucial movements, the historic experiments, the pivotal skills which are like the jewels in a watch or the intersections of a city. The importance of knowing a trade has always been recognized; it is one way of becoming complete in manhood. It is not the only way, as some fanatics would have it. But the imagination is necessary here as elsewhere; the imagination, and the sense it brings that real things are being learned.

The worst indictment against elementary education at present is that while it sends a minority on to better discipline it leaves the mass of us able to instruct and amuse ourselves only with the cheapest press in history. The indictment is heard every day, nor is it a new one. Thoreau said: "Our reading, our conversation and thinking, are all on a very low level, worthy only of pygmies and manikins. We are underfed and low-lived and illiterate"; we threaten to become a "race of tit-men." But Thoreau was saved the spectacle of newsstands smeared with thousands of periodicals so depressing in their sameness and so lethal in their poverty of word and thought that we may well question the future of any society which feeds upon them. If ours does so nourish itself, elementary education is partly to blame. The population of no age is perfect in taste and judgment. But the common intellect can be debauched, and superstition never did a more vicious job at this than the spurious literature of the newsstand is prepared to do. A generation trained in better operations of the reason and the hand, the imagination and the eye, would insist on better pleasures. The mind with nothing in it but fair memories and fixed relations knows indeed how to please itself. In a millennium there would be millions of such minds.

The "children" in the discussion just ended were not infants merely. They were all those whom education considers before it ascends to become liberal. They were the students of schools, low schools or high schools according as terminology decides. The distinction between them and adolescents—individuals in the process of becoming persons —whose natural need is for discipline in reason, has less to do with institutions than with the stages of life. A controversy roars at the moment over the age at which liberal education should begin. It is probably younger than our institutions recognize, and the high school may have to adjust itself to the fact, either by disappearing or by distributing its effort—backward into the grammar school, to make that better than it is, and forward into the college, to make it freer than at present to assume that the elementary job is thoroughly done. The prime distinction is between school and college. They stand respectively for elementary and liberal education, and clarity on this point would prevent much argument. The current argument is not embraced in this book, which must confine itself to education as such, whenever and wherever it happens.

Since the college is to have the next and longest chapter to itself, it will only be glanced at here in the interests of perspective. It is "the school of mankind," a place where he who was a child begins his study of the rules by which he may become a citizen in the republic of human understanding. Ideally it is an institution in which all men are viewed in their effort to be the same man; in which they will be seen of course to fail in so far as individuals necessarily differ, but in which difference shows against a background of definition. Definition occurs when all study the same things, and when these things are important. Only then does difference reach the high and exciting level of personality. Human beings have to have something in common, and it had better be a definition of their single nature than the random tags, the last-minute clichés at which college seniors are sometimes reduced to clutch as they depart into another life. College graduates today tend to be uniform in their lack of common and leading knowledge. That is why they can disagree only about little things, and why public debate so seldom exposes principles.

College studies are the permanent studies, the studies suitable to that moment when, as Whitehead has said, the mind becomes "a regiment instead of a rabble"; when the useful and the poetic arts are seen together in a new light of seriousness, so that now the youth finds poetry to be of practical importance, and science a lever with which to lift the gates of the world; when tradition speaks with its first real authority, and a body about to become mature finds that it contains a mind for which history and morality have prepared rituals; when abstraction first delights, and speculation becomes a necessity so shameless that parents, witnessing its wayward agonies, do not know whether to be

[99]

terrified or amused; when, in short, the boy has the will to become the man.

The function of the college is to show him the way; to provide discussion rooms and laboratories where he may anchor his speculations in deeper exercises of the useful arts, so that poetry may grow for him into something more than vapors—though the vapors at some stage are precious too. The opportunity of the college is to open up the realm of reason, not as a mapped place where any tourist may go in comfort but as the least familiar of human regions, though it is a region where only men can feel at home. The youth can discover that one evidence of man's rationality is the thousand skills he possesses—not a visible evidence, for we cannot see a person deciding what is the next right thing to do; we only see him doing it. College is the place where youth first realizes how imperfect and yet how distinguishing the acts of reason are: the acts not alone of logic but of abstraction too, of seeing what does not change among all the things that do, and of manipulating objects in the light of ideas that have first been understood. College is not the final school. But it is the school which makes possible any end.

University studies are progressive studies. They are terminal in the sense that none exist beyond them, but in themselves they never end, for their goal of knowledge is always retreating as they advance. Liberal education is both an end in itself, as any human good must be, and a means to the end of university studies, which cannot be undertaken except by a mind which its owner knows how to use.

The better liberal education is, the better universities will be. They themselves need liberalizing now, and this is because their students are poorly prepared. Albert Jay Nock once asked whether our masters of arts deserved the title. "Are they showing disciplined and experienced minds, are they capable of maintaining a mature and informed disinterestedness, a humane and elevated serenity, in all their views of human life? Do they display invariably the imperial distinction of spirit, the patrician fineness of taste, which we have been taught to associate with that degree of proficiency in the liberal arts?" The answer, Nock meant, was no, and few among those who understand what he was talking about would disagree. When liberal education fails to master the arts of communication, university education fails to make the advances of which it is capable; and has no way of guessing what is meant by the advances it does make.

The liberal education we have does not send into the universities enough persons who are masters of their intellectual tradition. And the universities do little to correct the deficiency. A graduate student can begin and end his work in total ignorance of what the greatest poets, critics, philosophers, mathematicians, scientists, statesmen, and moralists have done before him. He thinks this does not matter, since the work he will do is new. It is work in a progressive study, but it will be new work only if he knows where the old stopped off; and even the progressive studies are not strictly new. They are the same studies as ever, intensified and specialized. When those who are devoted to them forget this, they have lost the distinction between advancing knowledge and marking time.

The ideal specialist is the fine end of education. "Mankind is naturally specialist," says Whitehead, and the popular notion agrees with him; the educated person is presumed to know particular things. So he does, and the point where his general education passes into his special education is hard to see. In a sense, good education is always both general and special. We should not want to learn if we did not believe we would know particular things; and on the other hand, the desire to know is what makes us submit to the disciplines of learning. But the specialist is rarely ideal. His activity these days has been compared by John Dewey to "the busy work of children." He is not so much a specialist as a pedant.

Descartes has said of pedants that they are "less capable of reasoning than they would have been had they never learned at all." What they learned was everything except the nature of their subject matter, its excuse and its genius. "The animal is a specialist, and a perfect one," but it does not know that. The ideal specialist is less perfect, but he knows what specialism means. It means the use of a good mind in the interest of things which are good to know. On every level of his education, from the elementary to this one of the university, his devotion has been double: to the arts of knowing, and to things waiting to be known. It still is double, though the form it now takes is the form of understanding, even while he peers at particulars, the setting they have in what Locke called "the order, rank, and beauty of the whole intellectual world." His particulars are not quite everything for him, since he perceives that the sum of all things known by specialists could never be equivalent to the truth. He may work alone but he is not isolated, for his devotion is to truth everywhere.

The university student's thesis is rarely challenged until it is finished. That is one right time to defend it, but another would be before he had written a word. He should be made to say what knowledge it will add to what other knowledge, and why it is good that this should be done. An educated person knows what he is doing. This is why scholars convene at Christmas and tell one another what they are up to, and become as philosophical as they can about their trade. If they succeed less often than they might in telling the world what it is they do—for the world deserves to know—the reason is that their interest in truth is less absolute than that of ideal specialists would be. The ideal specialist is proud when he can popularize his knowledge, for this means that he knows what it is. The more ordinary scholar leaves it to quacks who misquote him, so that if knowledge has been advanced we get only a garbled notion of where and how it arrived.

There is a fourth level of education which another volume than this would be needed to describe. It is the highest and widest of all, though the present provisions for it in our society could by no courtesy be called handsome. It is the level of adult education. "The things taught in colleges and schools," says Emerson, "are not an education, but the means of education." It is essential that the means be good, and that is why liberal education should be the constant study of responsible men. It is no less essential that they be used throughout the decades of life which can illuminate their purpose. It is only as we grow older that we learn why we have learned. The mind now takes on its meaning. Liberal education is justified.

Adult education, however, is ideally occupied with both the permanent and the progressive studies. The permanent ones can never be pursued too far; there is no danger that the college will have exhausted them. It has been said that no study is proper in college which cannot be continued through a long life, and there is evidence in the institutions of adult education we now have that liberal studies are still the most popularly sought. The doubts of their utility one may have entertained in college are dissipated by experience; or a poor training in them is to be repaired; or a complete lack of them is to be made up. Whatever the reason, adult education continues to be in large part liberal education; though when Thoreau wrote that "it is time villages were universities, and their elder inhabitants the fellows of universities, with leisure—if they indeed are so well off—to pursue liberal studies the rest of their lives," he described neither his own time nor this one. Adult education is so far from universal that millions of people are unaware that it exists.

There are no sabbaticals for all, seventh years in which every citizen may refresh his understanding either of his own trade or of the life common to men everywhere. As citizen and as person he can still afford to learn: to catch up with ideas he has missed, to become acquainted with new ones, to unlimber his soul for the career which remains. He particularly needs refreshment in his own specialty, which for him is the cardinal progressive study. The best way to get this is to be relivened in its theory, which now he is ready for the first time to consider in its broadest aspect. As things go, he must be content with courses which teach new tricks of the trade—the latest dodges and devices, psychological or mechanical. These have their immediate use, and the halls of adult learning are potentially so vast that there should be ample room for them. But there is the further need of the pleasures peculiar to deep and original thought concerning what one does. A sabbatical might be the time when rich and difficult books about one's calling could be thoroughly read. Such books are more than refreshing; they are relaxing in a degree that out-of-the-way works seldom are. To think more after years of thinking less is being born again.

Such sabbaticals for everybody are remote, but they are no more preposterous than the annual vacation must once have seemed. As a vacation gets us through the remaining months, so a seventh year of leisure might get us through the years. And it might get modern society through certain centuries which are the subject of prophetic brooding. It may be only adult education, conceived on a gigantic and liberal scale, that can bring the world commonwealth into being.

VI

The Idea of a College

THE FUTURE of American education, like its past, is bound up with the institution we know as the college. The American college is the one place where liberal education can keep its heart whole. Whether this will be done depends, as always before, not only upon the faculties of colleges but upon their students, not only upon alumni but upon parents; and increasingly it depends upon the view of education that is held everywhere, in the general opinion no less than in the particular opinions of elected governments. What President Tyler of Amherst said in 1856 is still true despite many changes in the national circumstance: "Scarcely anything in America is more distinctly American than the relation between the colleges and the common people." By the common people was meant all the people. All the people still have the fate of liberal education in their hands.

The American college even of today is descended in a direct line from the seventeenth century college which prepared so many persons for the ministry. It prepared others for secular life, and all who studied in it can be said to have been prepared for life. But its connection with religion was crucial; it was one way in which the deeper spirit of the time received expression. The college of today finds itself in a world not only secularized to the root but busily occupied with details of trade, profession, and technique. The question of its survival has everything to do with the question whether so busy a time possesses anything that could be called a deeper spirit. Doubtless it does, but it must be deep indeed, for few can define it. It is nothing a college can create, at least out of nothing. It is something, however, for which education can search and to which it can be sensitive. The American college of any time must belong to that time, but it is not expected to sink out of sight beneath a million details of which it considers itself only one. The ancient obligation of the college is to express, and to that extent to be, a living principle.

Roughly a hundred years ago the college in America found a new sky over its head. The European university was imported, bringing all that is now signified when we speak of graduate or professional education. The need for this was real, but its growth was so rapid and immense that the college to this day has not learned its right relation to it. The elective system was a desperate attempt to prepare college students for the multiplying careers of a higher education which with every decade changed its form. Meanwhile, and as a natural result of this failure to maintain its native integrity, the college found that it had another rival. Elementary education, in the form of the high school or the preparatory school, was reaching up to take over the liberal function which the college seemed ready to abandon. But either this was done badly or in turn the schools became little centers of preparation for special callings and careers.

In any case the college was confused, and with certain modifications it remains so. This means confusion everywhere; for liberal education, with which the college had been identified and with which nothing else has identified itself, is the nervous system of any world it serves. At least one reason for the present state of our nerves may be the state of liberal education—or, in America specifically, the state of its colleges.

THE CURRICULUM

The college is meaningless without a curriculum, but it is more so when it has one that is meaningless. What things shall be studied, in what order? A system of education which avoids those questions and concentrates on the problems of administration or teaching method, or which broods in public upon the metaphysics of student life, has lost its aim. All other problems are solved when the problem of the curriculum is solved; student life, for instance, becomes the life of study. Whatever the limitations of Herbert Spencer may have been, no one can sensibly disagree with him concerning "the enormous importance of determining in some rational way what things are really most worth learning." No one? Yet many educators do disagree with him. For the curriculum is not something which it is fashionable to ponder; and as for being rational about it, few oddities are more suspect. The problem itself is given up as hopeless, or at any rate as one for which there is "no time." That is to say, it is not accepted as a real problem. Were it so accepted, and its importance granted, its solution might be within the bounds of likelihood.

The reality of the problem was dealt its worst blow by the elective system, which most educators now damn but which few know yet how to disarm. It seems to have been conceived as a device to ensure the natural sciences, so mistakenly feared and fought by the "humanities," their proper place among the liberal studies where they belonged. If the tactics failed, the reason was not so much that the classics which gave battle were too narrow in their outlook, or that the old war between humanism and science was erroneous, as that liberal strategy had been lost. The curriculum was now completely flexible, but it had no joints. It was open, but it did not know what to contain. The classical education of a century ago deserved and got its criticism. The education that took its place, substituting for the three disciplines of Latin, Greek, and mathematics a hundred subjects for none of which the discipline can be named, deserved—and recently has got—a harsher criticism still. It is charged with having confused breadth with variety. Wanting "something of everything," it is said to have got "nothing in the end." Incapable of its own synthesis, it hoped that the student would find his; yet countless observers have reported the student as anything but happy in the adventure. "The final result is apathy or intellectual and emotional paralysis," the only positive expression of which takes the form of snap judgments about everything.

Such criticism is hard on the student, who often merits a better word, but it is not too hard on the system which neglects his good. That system is liberal in the weak sense, not the strong; the freedom of the student comes not by discipline but by default. Almost nowhere is a balanced education available to him, nor is he encouraged to seek it for himself. He is offered ideas galore, but in the inert form which attends them when they are untested by other ideas. Vital knowledge may be there, and teachers may exist who could assist him in the still more vital business of its organization. He finds it, however, and finds the teachers, only by accident, during the course of expeditions which themselves consume his energy. Liberal education is difficult at best, and the student must do most of the work. This does not mean that no one should tell him what the work is.

Until he is told, he will have to be content with the self-education which a capable youth can still secure from whatever institution surrounds him. If this institution is a university from which his college hangs as an appendage, he has many riches within reach. But such an education is next-best, for it is bound to lack symmetry. Meanwhile he must make of it what he can, guided by such principles of search and selection as are given him by chance elders or his own intuition.

The elective system has long been under fire, but the aim of its critics is still uncertain and their spirit is irresolute. They suspect as illiberal the person who acts as if he understood what liberal education is. He may be wrong, but they do not expose his error; they only condemn his effrontery in claiming to know his business. Least of all do they tolerate in him the disposition to say that if liberal education is, it is the same for everybody; that the training it requires, in addition to being formal, should be homogeneous through four years—if the best is known, there is no student whom it will not fit, and each should have all of it.

The search for a curriculum is the search for one that is worthy to be uniform and universal. Such a curriculum is the end of any serious thought about liberal education.

Liberal studies are by definition studies which we "are not at liberty to omit." An educated society is one whose members know the same things, and have the same intellectual powers. The search of the educator should be for those things, and for the comprehension of those powers. If to say this is to raise the specter of a system so stable as to be dead, the answer is that stability does not consort with death. Its prime condition is experiment; and historically it is true that when there was the most argument among educators, provided they had a common ground for disagreement, education went farthest ahead. The best example of a dead or static situation is the one with which we are beginning to be discontented. Contemporary educators have disagreed, but not about essentials, for these have rarely been discussed. There is no danger that they will ever be discussed too well.

The job for educators during the days ahead is a job of discussion. No curriculum will emerge unless this discussion is constant and fundamental. But the one thing necessary for that is a common desire among teachers, corresponding to a common desire among men, for the clearest obtainable notion as to what the human mind can be and do. In proportion as this desire is common, the debate will be excellent and lively. The best circumstances would be those in which several men who were already engaged in educating one another, as friends do, met regularly in search of a rational curriculum. These might be the faculty of a given college, or the core of such a faculty. Talk of the sort does happen, now as at any time, but it is rarely responsible talk. The hope is that in every college it should become responsible, and that sooner or later all members of the college should come into it. For only then can there emerge a curriculum worth defending; one that all the teachers will understand with singleness of mind, and one for which students may grow up to be grateful. Indeed, there is little hope for liberal education in America unless such consummations occur; unless the colleges know themselves, and eventually know one another.

The discussion must be fearlessly fundamental. No question is too embarrassing to be asked. Some studies seem to have been inherited from a past which nobody remembers; should they be kept, and why? The question is to be answered only after the past has been explored, but no function of the discussion is more important than that; to know itself, education needs to know its history. And of the studies which are kept, what is to be the order? Have they a hierarchy of excellence? How do they group themselves, and what are the relations between the groups? It has been said that there is no ideal education, but the discussion should not hesitate to be ideal—the most practical thing education can ever be. And it should be conducted well; the discussion itself should be a work of art, a work of liberal art. If the teachers are not yet liberal artists, they will have to become so. This will take time, but so will the entire enterprise; centuries may not be too long. Nor does the result have to be a series of revolutions or clean sweeps. Whatever is good should be kept, just as whatever is rotten should be thrown away. Neither does the prescription call for a battle royal between divisions or departments, each bent upon surviving at whatever bloody cost. The end is the good of all. The faculty of one college, pausing to do this now, and doing it responsibly, might change the future course of education. Good thought, like courage, is contagious, and will not stop short of the world's end.

Such talk would mean among other things that teachers taught each other. There is no more perfect situation than that; though the suggestion that it be done is not invariably popular, since many teachers took their degrees with the thought that they were thus protected forever against intellectual challenge. Good teachers do teach each other, naturally and continuously; and this is the next best thing —for one situation is still nearer the perfection now being contemplated—to their all teaching all of the things the student learns. The student's mind is a gathering place, and every teacher's mind might be this also. But it will be a long time before teachers have the bravery to extend their knowledge beyond the specialties they started with. A truly coherent curriculum demands that they should, and in some millennium they may.

For the present it must suffice if in their colloquies they show as unified an understanding of their curriculum as is possible from its outside. The first sign of such an understanding would come when they agreed that the subjects to be taught should be few, not many. There are too many now, with the result that college "offerings" are speciously broad. When they are apparently narrow but actually deep, they will have that spreading power which education desires.

The search must be for a narrow formula—wisely narrow, of course; or, if the word is not outworn, creatively narrow. The only classification of studies that is capable of interesting the mind is a simple classification, under a few heads: three or four at the most. And these had better be the right ones, or the liberal arts will take their revenge. The average list of "subjects" currently taught "is a rapid table of contents," says Whitehead, "which a deity might run over in his mind while he was thinking of creating a world, and had not yet determined how to put it together." A curriculum creates a world. It is important then that it have a center and an order of parts. Some studies are surely secondary to others, as some rest on others as a base. This should be made manifest, and no student should be permitted to ignore the primary, the basic matter. The problem, as T. S. Eliot has pointed out, is spiritual; which does not make it postponable to some future date. But it is also psychological. Studies have their own natural joints, their relations to one another of sequence and of difficulty; the cutting up should then be done by persons with a kind of surgical knowledge, not by "curriculum butchers," to borrow a cruel but current epithet.

The skill required is more, of course, than surgical, it is philosophical. A better figure might be stolen from the art of fire-building, where it is essential that the kindling, the backlog, the front log, the green wood, the dead wood, and the layer of sustaining ashes be so disposed that a draft is possible at all times. The fire then spreads by natural stages, and is always intenser than it had been. Perhaps the philosopher can best lay the fire of the curriculum; and this suggests that all teachers should work to be philosophers, at least in their conferences about the college. Nothing encourages them at present to aim at this felicity. Philosophy is something that one department teaches, just as religion is encountered only in parochial schools. Philosophy is the first need everywhere. It is the free space that keeps the fire burning; it is the draft and not the damper. We shall refuse to believe in the seriousness of curriculum makers until we hear that they have decided, in the interests of philosophy, not to leave departments of philosophy in being. This would prove that they recognized the role of ideas not only in education but in such work as the world itself gets done.

"The world is a wedding," said some scholar of the Talmud. He did not proceed and specify, so the remark can mean anything one pleases. At this point it can mean that the world is one thing made from several joined together. The parties to a marriage are one, as everybody knows; but if they were literally one the statement would not have life. Education sees the world as a wedding of several parties, none of which loses identity in the process, but all of which remain connected. The connectedness of things is what the educator contemplates to the limit of his capacity. No human capacity is great enough to permit a vision of the world as simple, but if the educator does not aim at the vision no one else will, and the consequences are dire when no one does. "There is a great central focus," said Renan, "in which poetry, science, and morality are identical, in which to know, to admire, and to love are one and the same thing." He said this at twenty-five, and later he lost some of his illusion, but if his thought ever became important it was because he once had found a focus for it.

The student who can begin early in his life to think of things as connected, even if he revises his view with every succeeding year, has begun the life of learning. The experience of learning is the experience of having one part of the mind teach another, of understanding suddenly that *this* is *that* under an aspect hitherto unseen, of accumulating, at an ever-accelerated rate, the light that is generated whenever ideas converge. Nothing that can happen to men is more delightful than this, and it is a pity when it does not happen to them as students. To all but a few students today it cannot happen. There are gaps or breaks for them, as for their professors, between poetry and mathematics, between science and ethics, between philosophy and politics; their advance through these "subjects" is not on a single front; they do not study proportion as something equally present in arithmetic, in geometry, in architecture, in music, in physics, in the human body, and in poetry where its name is metaphor; they do not study form as something common to mathematics, metaphysics, and morals; they do not study tragedy as a process in ideas parallel to the course of calamity in the lives of persons. If they did, their leisure hours—so necessary to the studious career—might themselves possess a center, and the work unconsciously done in idleness might have results worth waiting for.

Doubtless all studies are one study in the end. But we do not know its name, and meanwhile we must be content with several names we have for its parts. Even these names vary, as do our conceptions of the parts. The main thing is that they should be few, and a favorable sign of the times is that discussion is already trying to reduce their number. No one suggests that Jefferson's three categories, dictated by the faculties of memory, reason, and imagination, be revived; or that the three philosophies—natural, mental, and moral—be restored in their ancient form. But three is not a bad number to aim at, and in fact the rational divisions proposed today are rarely more than four: history, literature, mathematics, and science. The number itself is not essential. A single distinction between the arts and the sciences might be enough. Or there could be an ordering of studies from the near to the remote: from the facts of life as found in poetry and history to the less apparent laws of science, and finally to the pure processes of mathematics. This would be an order of ghostliness, yielding in the end something like a definition of spirit—which, since it appears in poetry too, and doubtless in history, might be seen finishing its circle.

Any list might do if it respected reality, and if it led the student by some straight path through the liberal arts as in series they expose the forms of human knowledge. The forms, and of course the knowledge itself; by which is meant a great deal of particular knowledge, as necessary as numbers and as prescribable as the alphabet. The professor of physics who under the elective system urged his best undergraduates to "take" other things while they had time for them was not unwise. He was wrong, however, when he indicated that it did not matter what they took. The other things have their hierarchy too, though the elective system does not say so; and a genuine curriculum will permit no student to miss any important thing anywhere; the whole of it will be prescribed, and prescribed for everybody.

The knowledge must be more than particular. It must be firsthand. "Sampling and surveys" will not do. Jacques Maritain has made a useful distinction between knowledge about things and knowledge into them. The divisions into which certain institutions group their studies are little improvement upon the old departments if they stand for nothing better than introductions to fields of subject matter. Such language is unreal, and even the most glorified sampling must in the end be superficial beyond the benefit of what is called—as if it were a separate thing to be added at a separate time—integration. The knowledge of the student must be into things, and one at a time. Newman speaks of a certain "spurious philosophism" in education which he calls "viewiness," because it teaches nothing "soundly or thoroughly" but goes in for "brilliant general views about all things whatever." Antidotes, he says, are grammar and mathematics, chronology and geography, and metrical composition; but above all the medicine for a student is "the habit of method, of starting from fixed points, of making his ground good as he goes, of distinguishing what he knows from what he does not know." Such treatment is heroic because it is hard, but it is necessary if the student's practice is to be intelligent and if his theory is to be self-understood. The medicine is best administered in laboratories where thinking can be done through the refractory medium of things; and not only scientific laboratories, but laboratories in the arts, in history, in philosophy, and in mathematics. If no such laboratories are available, they must be conceived. Knowledge is not knowledge until it operates.

THE LIBERAL ARTS IN ACTION

The curriculum, as its name makes clear, is one course if it is not one study. It is the course over which the student moves as he masters the liberal arts. The knowledge necessary to such progress remains to be surveyed, but first to a few formal considerations.

"He who is ignorant of what happened before his birth," says Cicero, "is always a child." The reference was to history, but the sentence can be understood as taking in a richer thing, a thing richer even than "the culture which each generation purposely gives to those who are to be its successors." Mill's reference also falls short of the thing we call tradition. Tradition is so indispensable that it is regularly underrated, like other indispensable things. It is the medium through which we understand one another when communication takes place. It is the only way we have of knowing what we are. It is "the truth," says a metaphysician, "as it appears to human beings in time." And it is the prime occupation of a college, since that is the point where for the growing person past meets present and the two settle their differences.

If men were angels they could dispense with tradition, for they would know things all at once; and if they were animals they could do nicely with instinct as a substitute. Men must learn, and learn painfully, by accumulation and in time. The human tradition which collects this learning is more than history, and it is more than culture as culture is currently conceived. It is the ideas we have when we do not know we have them; it is the phoenix nest of language; it is the immortality in whose name education offers to secure the salvation of persons. It is what leaves novelty possible, in science or in art, for it marks the end from which beginnings can be made. Without it there can be no progress of any sort, and a civilization dies.

Tradition is dangerous to the intellect which does not know how to love it, for it can weigh heavily upon weak heads. To accept it is to borrow trouble, for it heaves with controversies and unanswered questions. It has been said that to inherit the tradition of democracy is like inheriting a lawsuit, and this goes for tradition in general. But tradition is most dangerous, and most troublesome, when it is forgotten. It gives strength as well as takes it. It brings life as well as threatens it. It is life fighting to maintain itself in time. For there is the curious fact that tradition is never so healthy as when it is being fought. We deny its authority, but in doing so we use its clearest terms; and end, if we are original, in enriching it so that it may have strength for future wars. It is orthodoxy at its best, thriving on heresies which it digests into nobler problems. We return to tradition not for answers but for questions, and some of those we find are capable, like live wires, of shocking us into a condition of dizziness or extreme heat. It is dangerous, and it is to be feared. But it fears us as well. The hope of education is to reconcile the two strengths.

The reconciliation is through discipline—another word whose definition involves paradox. There is an inverted romanticism about discipline which takes pleasure in contemplating its pains, but its joys are what matter. Discipline is desirable; indeed, it is craved by all who want wisdom out of their experience, or ability out of their acts.

It is the fashion now to make fun of what used to be called "formal discipline" in education. The theory of formal discipline is that certain studies if properly pursued yield not only knowledge of their own content but an intellectual skill which can be employed to advantage in other studies; it is the theory that certain studies are good for the mind. As a theory it was often expressed naïvely; and it was sometimes used in defense of studies for which nobody could discover the reason. But its bad name today can be traced in part to the fact that few living persons have submitted themselves to the sort of discipline under dispute. And the rest of the argument is off the point. For to maintain either that a study yields nothing but discipline or that it yields no discipline at all is to assume that all studies are hopelessly unrelated. Once a relation is assumed, then one study helps another as truth helps itself. Intellectual activity is more than the application of knowledge, it is the search for truth; and truth found anywhere will have its affinities in other fields. A truth possessed is itself a kind of training, since it teaches us how to recognize reality.

Even on the old terms the theory made more sense than it is given credit for. Formal discipline suggests definiteness, and in the hands of certain teachers it must have meant subtlety too. In so far as it signified the formation of intellectual habits it touched the central activity of learning. "Certainly," says Milton, "discipline is not only the removal of disorder, but the very visible shape and image of virtue." Discipline is not a policeman. It is a teacher, and indeed the only teacher without a fault. Scott Buchanan has measured its unique authority in a remark about college athletics—the one place, he says, where form means something to every student. Students will have their discipline whether or no, if only in the context of breath and muscle. The opportunity of the college is to provide it within the gates. The philosophers of a curriculum could make no graver error than to accept the fashionable criticism of formal discipline at its face value. It is superficial criticism, especially when it alleges that the powers acquired are trivial. The accuracy which mathematics requires is not a trivial virtue. But mathematics, particularly if it is enjoyed, also trains the mind in abstraction, the prelude to a central and major virtue. Particularly if it is enjoyed. For there is no disciplinary value in a study that is not taught and learned with relish. When there is excitement, then discipline becomes a privilege.

Both discipline and freedom are natural human desires, and each throws light upon the other. Men cannot be free unless their minds are free, but it is discipline that makes the mind free to realize its choices, to discriminate among them and determine their practicability. The free mind is "in charge of its knowledge." Since most of its knowledge sleeps in tradition, its first task is to establish a wakeful relation with that past which never dies; a relation outliving the original fear that freedom is lost in such a relation rather than certified. The task thenceforward is through discipline to acquire the freedom necessary for doing things well.

The undisciplined individual is free only to do things badly. Untrained in tennis, he is free to miss every shot. Untutored in the strings of a violin, he is licensed to produce hideous sounds. A barbarian in the arts of the trivium, he is untrammeled as he proceeds to misunderstand others and mislead himself. He may have feared that logic would make him a slave. But to what? It is lack of logic that keeps us helpless in a world where thought goes on whether we like it or not, and goes on less well if we cannot contribute to it; it is ignorance of language that makes us our own fools. As the useful arts free the body, and as the moral virtues free the appetite, so the intellectual virtues free the person in understanding and discourse. The freedom of the intellect gives us possession of our last and greatest powers, the powers most characteristic of us as men. That these powers had been unsuspected renders their possession all the more miraculous. That their exercise had been undesired—for there is an instinct in the animal man which coaxes him to avoid thought if he can—makes them the more lovable now. They are deep waters which must be "drilled and blasted for." And they have their unshakable authority, the conditions of their gift are not to be altered. Intelligence makes us free. "But that does not mean," says Alexander Meiklejohn, "free from intelligence."

Freedom is personal or not at all. It is achieved by those whose dignity deserves it, and it cannot be achieved without the discipline of knowledge. "The mind cannot be forced to believe what it knows to be false," says Pascal, "nor will to love what it knows must make it unhappy." In either case there is something to be known. Without such knowledge we cannot govern ourselves. We may be protected by laws from invasion of our external rights, but if we cannot protect the rights of our nature there is no power to which we can appeal. It is up to us to know our nature. And we had better be secure in this knowledge before we attempt either to free or to govern others. We cannot bestow a freedom we do not have ourselves; imitation freedoms will return as tyrannies to plague us, and orders that we impose will last no longer than the order within us. Only a monster will refuse to desire freedom for the world, but only a master of himself—and in the language of education this means a master of the liberal arts—will have any chance to achieve it.

Anyone is free to choose among the alternatives before him. Education, however, can increase the number of those choices, and liberal education can make their recognition positive. The worst artist knows least well what things he is free to do, and has the poorest equipment for making decisions. The courage to make decisions, and so to risk failure on the heroic or tragic level, is something else that depends upon knowledge; or, if the word seems deficient in warmth, upon wisdom. Wisdom is the final sign that we have become natural; that our decisions are our own, and that our allegiances are compulsive because personal. The courageous man appears to obey an instinct; it does not seem hard for him to do what for others would be impossible. But it was not easy for him to become this man. For one thing, he had in his youth to be active in studies the rewards for which were then only partially visible. And always he had to learn that independence of mind comes with willingness to understand others, with freedom from the fear of agreeing with them when they are in the neighborhood of truth, with clarity as to objects of all orders. The free mind is least jealous of its freedom; which is why courage seems to have no thought for itself, and why intelligence is required to distinguish it from rashness. It is also the reason that some men can give themselves to causes with no sense of personal surrender. They know what they are giving, and what they are giving it for. This is freedom gained, not lost.

The ability to be explicit in recognitions is a consequence of skill with respect to the universals of the same and the other. The liberal artist is a connoisseur of differences. Comenius would have had the child at its mother's knee trained in all the universals: "Something, nothing, it is, it is not, thus, otherwise, where, when, like, unlike, etc., and these are nothing but the prime concepts of metaphysic." If this seems too much for any child to do, the answer of Comenius would be that children do it anyway; the universals are all about them from the moment they begin to think and see. The universals are the simplest as well as the profoundest stuff of thought, and there is no such thing as too much skill in them, or too early skill. The mark of a mind is its capacity to make distinctions: to see them first, and then to state or use them. "He who distinguishes well," said Comenius, "is a good teacher." The universals of the same and the other, the like and the unlike, are at the bottom of learning.

Education might consider its best gift to be the gift of an artistry in difference. The student may be grateful who has been trained to see distinctions in position, distance, color, form, and time; in size and significance; in excellence and justice. The stupid mind, unschooled in forms and limits, runs all things together; or else it is baffled by what appears to it as an infinite series of individual things, ungrouped, unseparated. There is, to be sure, the intellectual who wearies us with distinctions he has invented out of nothing. These weigh the world down, and have no correspondence with the "divisions," as Locke called them, which "nature has placed in things." The question is less simple than Locke makes it, for nature and the mind are co-operative artists; the intellect half creates what it sees. Yet we do prefer the man whose distinctions refresh and liberate us, freeing us for further pleasure in our thought concerning the subject he has divided. Resemblances and differences are the starting places for poetry and speculation. They make the mind first come alive, and commit it to each of its acts.

No act of the mind is more delightful than the act of distinguishing persons from one another. "The greater intellect one has," said Pascal, "the more originality one finds in men. Ordinary persons find no difference between them." Ordinary persons, furthermore, expect others to be like themselves. The undistinguished mind misses distinctions. By the same token, of course, it misses resemblances; for the one thing cannot be perceived without the other. When gossip is intelligent it concerns itself with how so-and-so is the same as ever; his deeds run true to form. And one who relishes differences between persons equally relishes the classes into which they fall. The same and the different are inexhaustible subjects. Socrates could not have loved Alcibiades if Alcibiades had not been a man, and to that extent the same thing as himself; but the quality of his love depended also upon the difference he found between them, in age, in beauty, and in intellect. Some of a philosopher's friends are philosophers and some are not, and it is perhaps the latter whom he loves best, at least if they are much alive. "Who most deeply has thought," wrote the poet Hölderlin, "loves the most living." He had Socrates and Alcibiades in mind, but he spoke for anyone who thinks well, and in so doing discovers that the objects of thought are even more valuable than the best thought about them.

The liberal artist, mastering differences, must use among other things his imagination. "The soul," says Aristotle, "never thinks without images," and it is among images that distinctions are found. This does not look like that; these two are the same except here; between those three a thread of resemblance runs, even though it is almost, as Falstaff put it, invincible to thick sight. Such is the language of discrimination, which is a language both native and learned. Imagination is natural both in the sense that it cannot be invented and in the sense that it can be enriched by use and discipline. The more we think and feel, the better our imaginations are furnished. Passion and thought, says Emerson, work out "perpetual allegories" which the person both writes and reads within himself. The mind of man is only part intellect; it is also part sense, and the imagination is where these two teach other other. It is a power which we cannot always trust to give us the truth, for it is fallible, but without it the reason cannot be trusted either. If we could be sure it was wrong, we could be sure we were right. We trust it most in another when he seems wise, and yet it is an element of his wisdom. It has been called "the most intimately human faculty," which is why it is the hardest of all faculties to define. We do not know what it is, but we know when it is not there. And if it is not there, nothing of value is. It is no less necessary to the scientist than to the poet, to action than to thought. It is the power which education most steadily desires to perfect. Or should so desire. It is something that educators talk too little about, to our loss in happiness and truth.

Imagination always has work to do, whether in single minds or in the general will. It is the guardian angel of desire and decision, accounting for more right action, and for more wrong action, than anybody computes. Without it, for instance, the West can come to no conclusions about the East which war and fate are rapidly making a necessary object of its knowledge. Statistics and surveys of the East will not produce what an image can produce: an image of difference, so that no gross offenses are committed against the human fact of strangeness, and an image of similarity, even of identity, so that nothing homely is forgotten. The capacity for such images comes finally with intellectual and moral virtue; it is not the matter of luck that some suppose it, though single imaginations of great power are pieces of luck that civilization sometimes is favored with. It is a matter of training, of the tempered and prepared character which all educated persons can share. This character is a condition for the solution of any huge problem, either in the relations of peoples—and such relations, beginning at home, call first for knowledge of self, so that in the centuries to come it will be as important for the West to know itself as to know the East, which means to know itself better than education now encourages it to do—or in the ranges of pure speculation. In mathematics, for example, where imagination opens every new ceiling; in science, where it is the only faculty that can foresee the connections between things waiting in a world of mystery to be united; in literature, where nothing but itself can detect the possibilities of old meaning beneath the new materials of life; in religion, where it inspires the intellect to vast endeavors scarcely dreamed about today.

The arts of the trivium are never more important than at this point, and there is no better moment than this to consider how they might be managed in a curriculum. The question, rather, is how they might be viewed. Grammar, rhetoric, and logic are both one and three; they are a trinity, exclusive attention to one element in which yields poor discipline even there. It has already been said that the current practice is to teach them, when they are taught at all, in isolation from one another: logic as rules, rhetoric as tricks, and grammar as bald data. Each of them has a nobler and more liberal function when all work together. As one art they "mediate among the conflicting forces of experience: the actual world (grammar), the world of ideas (abstraction), and the world of imagination (rhetoric)." Those words are by a critic of our time who explains the low estate of contemporary literature by adding that "all modern action and all modern education are merely grammatical, with the result that anarchy has overtaken us even in the realm of the actual. The poet doesn't mean what he says: he only means his history and his times, or his semantic relation to society." Imagination and abstraction, the two realms where creation takes place, where originality resides, are dignified with no function, and so are left to atrophy. Logic is assumed to have no serious business outside of scientific method, and rhetoric becomes special pleading which cynicism can discount. The view, in other words, is of the intellect as a heap of parts; the whole has nothing single to do, and literature, to name no other art, loses most of its dimension.

This might explain why it is that poets are not expected to say important things, that rhetoric has a contemptible name, and that logic has shrunk to a device whereby we may catch an opponent in technical errors. The basic operations of the mind are not honored, either in performance or in idea. Perhaps it is not grammar that we have isolated, but rhetoric, which we call advertising. If so, we are an unfortunate people in that we despise the one art we license. We are not practical in our wisdom, or we would not countenance inconsistency at such a cost. The medium of rhetoric when seen as one of three sister arts is the medium of opinion, where wisdom consists in learning not only how to originate eloquence but how to respond to it, not only to speak honorably and well but to criticize those who fail or refuse to do so. Rhetoric these days is seldom credited with such a scope.

Logic, likewise, is reduced to an engine for ordering particulars, such as the facts of science. That is one of the disguises it is permitted to wear, but another is that of an angel ordering ideas. This disguise is at present less popular than the other, with the result that speculation has lost freedom and boldness. "The art of reasoning," says Whitehead, "consists in getting hold of the subject at the right end . . . of getting hold of the big ideas and of hanging on to them like grim death." This is a tough assignment, too ambitious for most contemporary logic.

It has been necessary to speak as generally as this about the arts of the trivium because they are omnipresent in the work of the mind. If somebody wonders how they should be "taught" in college, again the answer cannot be in terms of courses. Every subject has its grammar, or its data and its terms; its logic, or its reason for being among all the other subjects that are; and its rhetoric, or its capability of being stated. Proficiency in these arts will increase only with a belief in their importance, and with a dedication to the task of understanding their many relations in language and thought.

"It is apparent," remarks St. Augustine, "that only a very small measure of what a speaker thinks is expressed in his words." Language is something which the learned are said to overrate. Their own proficiency in it, we hear, makes them forget how much is apprehended by mankind in regions beyond expression, where principles are more than propositions, and where there is no existing language accurate enough to show what the mind means when it is most serious; our deepest assumptions are the ones we forget to prove, or realize cannot be proved. Not only are such things said of the learned; the learned say them too. They are true, but we should be on our guard against those who use language in order to deny its power. To do so goes beyond the truth that language is exactly as good as its user.

Some people can say more than others, and we should not ignore the fact. The great writers are those who have said the impossible. Before Shakespeare a great deal of the world did not exist. He made it exist, and it is quibbling to argue that the creation took place between his lines. It did take place, and words were the medium. So with lesser persons. Those who insist that they know what they think although they cannot say what it is should be invited to listen to others who can both think and speak. It is not easy to do both things, but some succeed. The learned habit of diverting our attention to rituals and patterns with which peoples have expressed themselves—in conduct, in song, in dance, in sacrament, in plastic structures such as huts and idols—leads us to important fields of truth. It is a habit, however, that rusts in us the wonderful mechanisms of communication by words. It is particularly sad when college students are told that no one ever expresses himself. Their ability to do so is poor enough as it is. It will not be augmented by eloquent sermons against eloquence.

Language can do more than say what men mean; it can say how they feel what they mean. It is a record of reason, but it also exhibits the person behind the reason. When that person speaks, kindling the words he uses with the flame of emphasis, other men will listen. We love the words of good writers and speakers; and our startled silence suggests that we think we have found good men. "A man's power," says Emerson, "to connect his thought with its proper symbol, and so to utter it, depends on the simplicity of his character, that is, upon his love of truth and his desire to communicate it without loss. The corruption of man is followed by the corruption of language."

If we do not believe in language today, the reason is that we do not believe in intellectual character. To acknowledge, as anyone must, that language is most valuable for the inexpressible realities it refers to is not to agree that it should be robbed of its power to refer. It gets this power by practice, and by a study of itself. If it is a mirror that reflects the truth, it needs to be kept "polished and adjusted" so that it can receive intellectual light with the least loss. That is why one's own language should be known as well as possible in terms of its peculiar genius; and why at least one other language—Greek is still the best one for the purpose, and indeed for any purpose—should be equally known. The lines of any two languages converge in the structure of language itself. Without a trained sense of this structure, reason is handicapped; and to the extent that it is handicapped, the imagination is barren.

Any language that exists has existed a long time, and its purpose is more general than the particular one we may wish to put it to. Even a new word, if we have not coined it, refers to something more general than the object before us. The art of using language, then, is the art of fitting garments of indefinite size to figures whose size is known. This is never easy; but it is especially difficult when the figure or object is one of those "great and precious things," as Plato has it, that "have no outward image of themselves visible to man, to which the teacher can lightly point and so satisfy the soul of the inquirer. Therefore we must train and discipline our minds to render and receive an account of them in words. For it can be done in no other way."

That is to say, we must be skillful in abstraction. The term is unnecessarily frightening in view of the fact that all thought is abstract when it is thought at all. Facts are more remote from our comprehension, unless it is trained, than ideas are; and the thing that trains us in the comprehension of facts is abstraction. But the term is feared and hated, especially by those who resist intellectual labor; though that is not the reason they give. They say they prefer reality, or experiment, or experience—themselves abstractions if abstractions ever were. They practice, in other words, the art they condemn; but practice it badly because they do not know they do.

"In the present age," said de Tocqueville, "the human mind must be coerced into theoretical studies." He wrote a hundred years ago, but that does not matter; our generation is like that. Indeed, any generation is, for at no time is the world populated by competent philosophers. But it does not hurt to have intellectual leaders who respect abstraction. Our teachers do not respect it. That is why they are cheerfully content to turn out students who all their lives will be theoretical without knowing it—will, that is, be weak in theory. John Dewey, who finds abstraction to be "the very artery of intelligence," says that it is "equivalent to taking the point of view of any man, whatever his location in time or space." He was speaking of scientific generalization, where abstraction flourishes today; nor in such a context is it feared and hated, for it is generally agreed that science should be difficult. But man is more than a scientist, and the rule should hold for all of his intellectual doings. As man he is abstract, and he is abstract everywhere. When he refuses to recognize this he misses much truth along with high pleasure. For few things are more charming than to feel warmth and light flood into terms that have hitherto seemed the cold, gray possessions of others. This can happen only when they have been studied in the faith that it is worth while to be accurate in their use. Then they cease to be what a contemporary metaphysician has called them, "beautiful colors in darkness."

The arts of the quadrivium have now a single name, which is mathematics. They are the arts of advanced discourse, dealing with a higher degree of abstraction than is ever explicit in the discourse presided over by the trivium. Their theme is quantity; though the Greeks, studying harmony in the fine arts, in ethics, in religion, and indeed in everything, made them a measure of quality too. Following the arts of the trivium as they do, they are subject to them as all other arts and studies are, and cannot afford to forget the fact. Their tendency, since in their further reaches they are progressive studies, is to cut their connection with the permanent studies and become esoteric. In their right relation they are indispensable, and must always be so.

Students who are permitted to elect against mathematics will remain ignorant of a mother tongue. Many persons believe they lack ability in this tongue, but in most cases the reason is that they have been taught it badly. For a majority to lack it might be to sacrifice the future of civilization.

This is not merely because mathematics is training in abstraction. It is that. But the question of formal discipline returns to vex those who would claim for mathematics nothing more than that it teaches something else. It has its own beauty, which is not fully described when we praise geometry, for instance, because it can accustom us to what Locke called long trains of consequences, and thus convert us into reasonable creatures. Scott Buchanan has indicated how much more there is to mathematics than that:

It is true that mathematics sometimes deals with rigid structures, chains, and networks, but they are not made of propositions, and long and elaborate arguments are most often bad mathematics. The structures with which mathematics deals are more like lace, the leaves of trees, and the play of light and shadow on a meadow or a human face, than they are like buildings and machines, the least of their representatives. The best proofs in mathematics are short and crisp like epigrams, and the longest have swings and rhythms that are like music. The structures of mathematics and the propositions about them are ways for the imagination to travel and the wings, or legs, or vehicles to take you where you want to go. The solemn sound of demonstrated mathematical truths is a professional way of announcing an arrival at some point on the journey fantastic. Let it be added for good measure that some of the greatest mathematical discoveries by the greatest mathematical minds have been theorems that they could not prove; some have never been proved. The fact of the matter is that anything worth discovering in mathematics does not need proof; it needs only to be seen or understood.

If teachers of mathematics are worried by such a compliment to their trade, students may not be, judging by the results of a questionnaire which 5,788 American high school pupils answered in 1923. Two per cent of them said they liked mathematics because it was "exact and definite," nineteen per cent because it was "good mental training," and twenty-two per cent because it was "useful"; but forty-one per cent said they liked it because it was "interesting." And only twelve per cent testified that it was "easy." It had been hard but interesting; the conditions for formal discipline have rarely been better stated. Nothing that is not discipline can be interesting long. But nothing that is not interesting can discipline the imagination where all studies take their start. This is not to judge studies by the appeal they make to random minds. The interest of the human mind is what matters, and it is assumed that education in every quarter is occupied with making the human mind aware of its desires.

Mathematics has its own beauty, and sometimes this beauty falls in love with itself. If it is the godlike science it has been praised as being, it can reveal a divine madness which expresses itself as the urge not to measure this world but to make another, to deal with symbols as if they were symbols of nothing. It can eat up the sciences which use it, provided their knowledge of themselves is weak enough, so that their ambition is finally to be identical with it. The great mathematical revolution of the seventeenth century still works in this way. The quadrivium, that is, shows by its triumphs over nature how unnatural art can be when it loses its bearings. If all of the arts are not one art, they nevertheless are partners in a universal enterprise.

The physical sciences are a problem for the educator because they do their work so well. They must be caught up with, if only to be subdued. But the way to catch up with them is not to sermonize against their inhumanity. The liberal arts survive more intact in their laboratories than elsewhere in education today; other studies, studying them, could learn about themselves. The word "truth" as scientists use it may have limited meaning, but it has meaning. "Not all the powers on earth can, by the force of authority, persuade us of a point of fact," says Pascal, "any more than they can alter it; for nothing can make that to be not which really is." The scientist may deal imperfectly with existence, but it is existence with which he deals, and his code of observation, classification, deduction, verification, and prophecy is almost unique in its disinterestedness. If he now does less thinking than the grandeur of his theme dictates, the reason is partly because he has lacked thoughtful partners in the enterprise of intellect. His famous method is left to run by itself, a machine which he himself fails to understand in proportion as others fail.

The student must have more than a verbal knowledge of science, just as science must attain in time more than an automatic acquaintance with itself. Nowhere do more ideas converge, and nowhere are the brain, hand, and eye more usable together. The useful arts grow philosophical in science. At least they do if a proper setting is prepared. In the contemporary college the setting is more lavish than liberal. The student in the laboratory is trained for a profession rather than educated for understanding, and he is picked for training as specialists are picked. His teachers are not liberal artists. If and when education makes them so, their desire will be that all students should master instruments and perform experiments; and not with research in view, but an education. For science is essential to education at the same moment that poetry and philosophy are.

The high hopes for science in the nineteenth century, when other disciplines were declining, have long since seemed absurd; though the other disciplines have not mended. Renan could believe at twenty-five that the poetry, morality, and myth which science had so far destroyed would be rebuilt by it into "a reality a thousand times superior." Science, unaided, has no such powers; and it has had little aid. "It is certain," said Huxley, "that nature is the expression of a definite order with which nothing interferes, and that the chief business of mankind is to learn that order and govern themselves accordingly." In any other context than that which is familiar to us, this statement could refer to the whole universe as man can know it; it does not sound, for instance, too different from Dante. But the modern context reduces it to a vision of matter and mechanics. The world created by seventeenth century mathematics and science was "hard, cold, colorless, silent, and dead," with a single order of truth which saw nature as neither passionate nor personal. Nature too is a person. But the "law of parsimony," as William James puts it, withers both world and man; it yields only "the leanest, lowest, aridest result." The world of modern man has been in consequence "little and plain, perspectiveless and short." It has been a world where scientists could be intellectually commonplace, and where their commonplaceness could infect the intellectuals about them. But the fault was mutual.

It was agreed too long that men could "rush into the examination of Nature as though they bore some proportion to her." So Pascal, whose lonely voice is more and more echoed of late. The certainties of science are widely doubted as it is seen that the modern scientist has been an inadequate philosopher. He has used philosophy because he could not do without it, but the specimens available to him were those that lingered by inertia in his mind. Scientists have tended to be children when they thought, nor was their thought commensurate with the problems attacked. Really to comprehend a fact might be to comprehend everything, for the meaning of anything is a related meaning. The scientist holds great power in his hands, but it may be a different kind from that which he claims it is, and it could be greater than he realizes. His daily doings are done in a void which his imagination has not been taught to measure. They will grow trivial if his conception does not enlarge itself, if his metaphysic fails to keep pace. He has a higher and a lower function, and they depend upon each other—the higher for speculation and insight, the lower for operation and demonstration. He will demonstrate less as his vision shrinks; or the amount he demonstrates will increase only as confusion and danger increase when we know not what we do.

The clearest proof of the scientist's intellectual immaturity has been his dogmatism. He probably despises the medieval schoolmen as his seventeenth century ancestors did, but there is no good answer to Whitehead's remark that "the sort of person who was a scholastic doctor in a medieval university today is a scientific professor in a modern university." He accuses everybody of dogmatism except himself, yet he is capable of that sin to an asphyxiating degree. When this is true, the reason is that he·does not know where his ideas come from, and whether they are good ideas. Ideas do not come from experiment. Their origin is the mind's experience, and the mind has many mansions. Philosophy should have told him so, but philosophy itself has been asleep. The business of the scientist is with idea and fact. He thinks it is with fact alone. But the mystic may be closer to facts than a manipulator of instruments can ever be. The instruments are necessary to civilization, but so are the things that can happen to the mind. The scientist takes the mind for granted. It is the last thing man can afford to take for granted.

The modern distinction between science and philosophy is both fortunate and unfortunate. Ideally it shows the way to a more perfect performance by each; in practice it has meant the public sacrifice of philosophy. The two should be mutual critics, but one has degraded the other; philosophy is in disrepute. This means that even science has lost dimension. When philosophy is dismissed as guesswork, science monopolizes judgment. When the good is known less well than things, said Socrates, then the value even of things is missed. The student should not be left in ignorance of the search that goes on, even if only in corners, for a philosophy of science. The college student will not discover this, or contribute to its discovery; but no time is too early to learn that the problem exists.

Philosophy has its own obligation to be humble. The deepest man has less reason than he desires, and reason at its best cannot reveal everything. Ideas do not always come when we call them. If philosophy is the science of sciences, it must be acknowledged that this queen of knowledge cannot know at first hand the plenum of existence; her dominion is distant. Science is selective, but so is she, though on a higher level of choice and certainty. For Plato she was the most exact of all the arts and sciences because she dealt with being, change, and truth. Such things are seldom said about philosophy today, or believed by philosophy itself, with the result that the cue of humility, like the cue of pride, is too faintly heard. A task can be so huge that the person to whom it is assigned may take pride in the stern command that he be modest.

Science deals with special experience, but the experience of the philosopher is common to mankind. To be rational is to be human, and there are premises explicit in all thought. Philosophy tries to be clear about these, on every level of their significance. To ignore them altogether—to say that philosophy has no work to do—is to be, if one is a student, an intelligent imbecile. "To a sound judgment," says Emerson, "the most abstract truth is the most practical," for without an idea of creation it will be impossible to understand such things as "language, sleep, madness, dreams, beasts, sex." It is not merely, of course, that man wants a system whereby to explain lists of things, long or short as the case may be. What is more desirable is a sense that the one great thing, the world, has as much meaning as can be found in it. The student by his very youth is prompted to such inquiries, but often he must improvise crude answers because departments of philosophy are concerned only with the history of their subject, or with the details of a method which they call scientific. They do not claim truth as their province, a province wherein dialectic has work to do by way of exploring conflicts between doctrines each of which stands on solid ground. For again the business of philosophy is less with the right answers than with the right questions.

Philosophy's most practical concern is with the ends of action, and here it is autonomous, for science cannot legislate among desires. The obligation to be scientific is something that ethics, not science, announces. No perfection of scientific method could produce the proposition that justice is good, or that wisdom is better than knowledge. If there is a science that studies what men should do, it is not the science we currently worship. It is the one we neglect when we neglect philosophy—which, however, as has been said enough times already, neglects itself. It has its own certainties, which the senses cannot measure and of which the unseasoned intellect never dreams.

The seasoned intellect long since has rejected as too simple the distinction conventionally made between man and the world. There is not one thing, man, and then another thing, the world. The two are somehow one. Man, understanding himself, to some extent will understand the world, just as knowledge of it must include a provision for himself. His desire to be at home in it is a desire to live with himself. It is not the same thing as himself, and yet if it is altogether alien it is nothing. The world has its "unbending objectivity," as if it did not care whether it were known or not, since knowing makes no difference to it. But so has man his nature which must be what it is, and which the world cannot alter. It is philosophy that speaks of such things, and tries to penetrate their mystery.

But religion penetrates further. It too acknowledges objectivity, yet on such a scale that the nature of things becomes infinitely less wonderful than their existence. Science and philosophy must rest in nature; their inquiry is confined to what things are and how they are connected, in number, place, and time. Religion goes on into the darkness where intellect must grapple with the original fact that things are at all. This is an overwhelming fact, for it measures our ignorance. Religion is the art that teaches us what to do with our ignorance. It does not teach us how to convert it into knowledge, for that cannot be done. But it shows us how we may dignify it with ritual, which is man's way of confessing his ignorance in a style suitable to its size. The worm does not confess the inferiority of its knowledge. Man can do so, and has erected the act into an art.

The first deed in religion is a deed of the imagination. The extent of the unknown is conceived. This is a conception which some universities are too proud to publish; with the result that they pass for omniscient, and so deserve the charge of a contemporary philosopher that they are liars. At any rate they are imperfect teachers, for they do not guide the student to the edge of that abyss where his imagination would receive its final discipline. They do not show him the darkness which would make his own light more brilliant by contrast than it now appears. There can be no such contrast when the unknown is denied.

If the student has no religion of his own, he will learn nothing in college from lectures about religion or from courses in its history. His imagination must act, stimulating his intellect to as many as possible of those subtleties which theology seems sometimes to cherish as a secret possession. He is not expected to become a theologian. He is not ordered to embrace a faith. But intimations of the experience are available to him, and it is a part of education that they should do their work. A single book, the *Pensées* of Pascal, will bring them as near to him as they can come without revelation. It has the advantage for his purpose of being one of the wittiest books in the world—and, in the candor of its remarks about man, one of the wickedest. It was written with sharp eyes by a great mathematician. That is why it can plunge so directly and cleanly into the abyss, and why it can be so convincing when it says that science and reason are insufficient. The famous seventy-second section, on "man's disproportion," will cut any sensitive intellect forever free from the superstition that man can be at home in a universe whose boundaries are two infinities. He can be stabled or bedded in his own house and barn, but even an education that wants to domesticate him in reality can only introduce him here to a reality whose rafters he will never see. That it should do so is necessary to his becoming a full man; which means that it should be done well, as Pascal does it, voyaging with intelligence between the terrible and the beautiful, creating with stroke after stroke of finest prose the image of the spirit's eternal predicament. Our indifference to eternity, says Pascal, is "an incomprehensible enchantment, and a supernatural slumber." It is the same thing as our indifference to the present, which ought to seem so tremendous a gift that we trembled with incessant doubt concerning our power to make the best use of it. Few of us do that, and it may be well. The student, however, should guess what it means to be visited by the anxiety.

As every man is a philosopher of sorts, so every man is a theologian if he can see beyond his nose. Our common refusal to admit this condemns us to use a good deal of traditional language without knowing it. If we knew it, we might either abandon or perfect its use. Most of our terms for man when we praise him are inherited from languages that traced his highest nature to the gods. Their nature fulfilled his, and still does in the words heroic, gracious, magnanimous, and elect; though if we do not know this we are but parrots. Liberal education, one of whose functions is to remind us what words mean, can present us here with two alternatives: that of silence, or that of becoming birds who know the music better. Owls, perhaps; but owls are wiser than parrots.

Liberal education is not responsible to religion. It never created one, and so, if another is needed now, liberal education will not be its source. Liberal education is occupied with the nature of things, and chiefly with the nature of man. At its distance, however, and by the hard way of intelligence, it comprehends religion. And it is prepared to explain why new religions sometimes take thousands of years to appear. Ideas of sufficient depth and generality require that much time to mature. Liberal education is addicted to ideas, even if it does not prophesy.

THE GREAT TRADITION

The medium of liberal education is that portion of the past which is always present. It consists of the liberal arts, literary and mathematical, because they control thinking whenever thinking is done; and equally it consists of the great works in which meaning has been given to the ideal statement that human life is itself an art.

If this is true, the curriculum for any college may be simply described. The four years of every student will be devoted to two principal and simultaneous activities: learning the arts of investigation, discovery, criticism, and communication, and achieving at first hand an acquaintance with the original books, the unkillable classics, in which these miracles have happened.

Neither activity is conceivable without the other. Once more, there can be no courses in the arts as such, however well they may be illuminated by lectures on them and by laboratory exercises, literary or mathematical, designed to reveal their structure and beauty. Such exercises would ensure that a student learned to read, write, measure, compare, distinguish, and identify. But such operations are not performed upon nothing. There must be materials, and the materials in this case are the best works of the best imaginations. But neither have the classics come out of nothing. They have enjoyed their supporting medium, just as they have become a kind of medium in themselves. The supporting medium is the great tradition of the liberal arts. That medium and what it contains, the bone and the marrow together, suggest that a curriculum already exists. It remains only to be rediscovered, and to be put into effect by teachers who know how discipline in language, literature, and science is best made lovable and so desirable, and who have that discipline themselves because they have mastered its medium. A given college can add as many extras as it has time for, garnishing the meat with parsley, thyme, or a hundred other savors. But the meat must be there, or there is no college.

The immediate task of educators is to convince themselves that the arts of language and the arts of science are equally and indeed mutually humane. Education suffers from the sense it has that one set of arts is more conservative and respectable than the other, and that it is being fought to extinction by the other set. If such a conflict were real it would destroy the world we have known. The arts of literature, religion, ethics, and politics are not to be thought of as holding out against science and mathematics. When they are so thought of, the reason is that science and mathematics are not understood as being and having art, as capable of ultimate refinement, as radical in the root sense of necessary, after the fashion of poetry when poetry is something better than a reservoir of decayed beliefs. "Language and mathematics are the mother tongues of our rational selves"—that is, of the human race—and no student should be permitted to be speechless in either tongue, whatever value he sets upon his special gifts, and however sure he may be at sixteen or eighteen that he knows the uses to which his mind will eventually be put. This would be like amputating his left hand because he did not seem to be ambidextrous. The languages of art and science are of twin importance. It is crippling to be illiterate in either, and the natural curriculum does not choose between them. They are two ways in which the student will have to express himself; they are two ways in which the truth gets known.

William Whewell, considering the curriculum of Cambridge University a century ago, concluded that to be without discipline in language is to be illiterate and that to be innocent of mathematics is to be irrational. The distinction is interesting but incomplete. Our trouble is worse than Whewell suggests. We are irrational artists and illiterate scientists; or at any rate this is true of the intellectual who is proud that he knows no chemistry, and of the technician who reflects his contempt for poetry in the childlike character of his moral and political opinions. The terrible example of Darwin, who used his mind like a machine until it lost the power to find Shakespeare anything but "intolerably dull" and "nauseating," and who knew too late that the penalty was "a loss of happiness," is an example on one side only. None so forceful has appeared upon the other side, though one is scarcely needed in a time when literary and philosophical careers atrophy so early, when intellectual movements are so short-lived and self-defeating, as if the field under cultivation were always too small; and when the opinions of soft intellectuals are ignored as systematically as those of the hard ones are admired.

Once again there is history behind all this. Bacon's twofold order of truth—truth in things and truth in words—has borne bad fruit; and the determination of Descartes to abandon the study of letters for an education in "the great book of the world" has done less for the world than he hoped, at the same time that it has withered poetry. The poet of an older time who assumed that he could know as much as any man—and half a dozen of his species did—exists no longer; while science more and more noticeably suffers from the all but universal conviction that it alone can deal with reality. The reality it finds is deficient in fancy and even in logic. The scientist who is proud of having no imagination does not realize that to this extent he lacks a mind. The poet, meanwhile, who ignores or abuses his intellect seems not to know, though the rest of the world does, that his imagination has grown feeble.

The relations seen by the scientist among parts would be seen better if he could imagine their whole, and the poet would feel the quality of this whole with greater strength if he were literate in its parts. The two disciplines are interdependent: the discipline of the poet, who starts from the facts of life, and the discipline of the mathematician, who wants to end there. It is superficial to say that science reasons and art feels. Each of them does both, because each of them to succeed greatly must be subtle with symbols. The modern poet is too conscious of his symbols; the modern scientist is too unconscious of his. We get too little knowledge from the poet, who understands only his own psychological processes, and too little light from the scientist, who understands everything except himself.

The great tradition tells how such a situation could and did come about, for the great tradition is among other things the history of intellectual events, at the same time that it contains in itself the cure. The classics of our world, the great books, ancient and recent, in which the Western mind has worked and played, are more essential to a college than its buildings and its bells, or even perhaps its teachers; for these books are teachers from which every wise and witty man has learned what he knows. They are the one accessible source of whatever ideas have existed and survived their times. To know them in their relations with one another, for they have a strong family resemblance even when they argue like contrary winds, is to re-enact the drama of human thought and feeling, and to be capable of assisting in new scenes. The common possession of the experience they offer would civilize any society that had it, not by stopping controversy but by giving it the new lease of a start which all could understand. The common ignorance of them which now prevails is why literature and science are both so unsatisfactory; and why so few persons think they are educated. The proposal to plant the classics at the center of the college curriculum is simple in the sense that it can be stated in one breath. But it calls for so much intellectual labor and good will that most educators prefer to spend enormous sums of energy in doing easier things. All other things are easier, however much more complicated they may sound. So it will take time to get the proposal accepted. Until it is accepted everywhere in America, we shall lack the right to say that liberal education exists among us.

There is no scarcity at present of courses, departments, and divisions which prescribe for students the reading of certain masterpieces in literature or in science. So far, so good. But such prescriptions are partial; the literary masterpieces are read separately from the mathematical, as if either half of the tradition were intelligible by itself. The tradition is one, even if its languages are two. The imagination is not split at its base. It is the human imagination, and it is one if man is one.

But there is one contemporary college whose entire effort is concentrated upon the reading, uniformly by all of its students through four years, of a list of great books which is so long and so excellent, and at the same time so arduous, that it might appear to exhaust the category. It scarcely does that, nor would anyone be wrong who supposed that this or any other list should be challenged and revised; the college in question does in fact continually revise it. But the heart of the tradition is there with its essential chambers, and it is kept working for all of the students all of the time. It is the end of every other activity in this college; languages are learned so that these books may be read, and among the languages are those of mathematics and the laboratory. There are no textbooks to which the great books are supplementary; the great books are the textbooks of this college, as in a sense they are its teachers. For the faculty reads them too, in preparation for seminars where they will be discussed. And since there are no departments or divisions, all of the faculty must do what all of the students do: read all of the books.

The curriculum of St. John's College in Maryland, to be specific, is as follows:

Homer: *Iliad* and *Odyssey*
Aeschylus: *Oresteia*
Herodotus: *History*
Sophocles: *Oedipus Rex*
Hippocrates: *Ancient Medicine* and *Airs, Waters, and Places*
Euripides: *Medea*
Thucydides: *History of the Peloponnesian War*
Aristophanes: *Frogs, Clouds, Birds*
Aristarchus: *On the Sizes and Distances of the Sun and Moon*
Plato: *Dialogues*
Aristotle: *Organon, Poetics, Physics, Politics*
Archimedes: Selected Works
Euclid: *Elements*
Apollonius: *Conics*
Cicero: *On Duties*
Lucretius: *On the Nature of Things*
Virgil: *Aeneid*
The Bible
Epictetus: *Moral Discourses*
Nicomachus: *Introduction to Arithmetic*
Plutarch: *Lives*
Tacitus: *The Histories*
Ptolemy: *Mathematical Composition*
Lucian: *True History*
Galen: *On the Natural Faculties*
Plotinus: *Enneads*
Augustine: *Confessions, On Music, Concerning the Teacher*
Justinian: *Institutes*
Song of Roland
Saga of Burnt Njal
Grosseteste: *On Light*
Bonaventure: *On the Reduction of the Arts to Theology*
Aquinas: *On Being and Essence, Treatise on God, Treatise on Man*
Dante: *Divine Comedy*
Chaucer: *Canterbury Tales*
Oresme: *On the Breadths of Forms*

THE IDEA OF A COLLEGE

Pico della Mirandola: *On the Dignity of Man*
Leonardo: Note Books
Machiavelli: *The Prince*
Erasmus: *In Praise of Folly*
Rabelais: *Gargantua*
Copernicus: *On the Revolutions of the Spheres*
Calvin: *Institutes*
Montaigne: *Essays*
Gilbert: *On the Loadstone*
Cervantes: *Don Quixote*
Shakespeare: *Henry IV, Hamlet, King Lear, Macbeth, Tempest*
Francis Bacon: *Novum Organum*
Kepler: *Epitome of Astronomy*
Harvey: *On the Motion of the Heart*
Corneille: *Le Cid*
Galileo: *Two New Sciences*
Descartes: *Geometry, Discourse on Method, Meditations*
Hobbes: *Leviathan*
Boyle: *Sceptical Chymist*
Molière: *Tartuffe*
Pascal: *Pensées*
Milton: *Paradise Lost*
Racine: *Phèdre*
Grotius: *Law of War and Peace*
Spinoza: *Ethics, Theological-Political Treatise*
Newton: *Principia Mathematica*
Locke: *Second Treatise on Civil Government*
Huygens: *Treatise on Light*
Berkeley: *Dialogues between Hylas and Philonous*
Leibniz: *Discourse on Metaphysics, Monadology*
Vico: *Scienza Nuova*
Swift: *Gulliver's Travels*
Hume: *Treatise of Human Nature*
Montesquieu: *Spirit of Laws*
Fielding: *Tom Jones*
Voltaire: *Candide, Micromegas*
Rousseau: *Social Contract*
Gibbon: *Decline and Fall of the Roman Empire*
Smith: *Wealth of Nations*
Kant: *Critique of Pure Reason*
Constitution of the United States
Federalist Papers
Bentham: *Principles of Morals and Legislation*
Lavoisier: *Treatise on Chemistry*

Malthus: *Principles of Population*
Dalton: *A New System of Chemical Philosophy*
Hegel: *Philosophy of History*
Fourier: *Analytical Theory of Heat*
Goethe: *Faust*
Lobachevski: *Theory of Parallels*
Faraday: *Experimental Researches in Electricity*
Peacock: *Treatise on Algebra*
Boole: *Laws of Thought*
Virchow: *Cellular Pathology*
Mill: *On Liberty*
Darwin: *Origin of Species*
Bernard: *Introduction to Experimental Medicine*
Mendel: *Experiments in Plant Hybridization*
Riemann: *Hypotheses of Geometry*
Dostoevski: *The Possessed*
Marx: *Capital*
Tolstoy: *War and Peace*
Dedekind: *Essays on Numbers*
Maxwell: *Electricity and Magnetism*
Flaubert: *Bouvard and Pécuchet*
Ibsen: *Ghosts, Rosmersholm*
Joule: Scientific Papers
James: *Principles of Psychology*
Freud: *Studies in Hysteria*
Cantor: *Transfinite Numbers*
Hilbert: *Foundations of Geometry*
Poincaré: *Science and Hypothesis*
Russell: *Principles of Mathematics*
Veblen and Young: *Projective Geometry*

If such a curriculum seems formidable, education is formidable. If it seems bare, that is because the beholder does not know the books. For one who knows them the mere list of their titles is a curriculum bursting with content, and a content with which no other can compare. Descriptions in college catalogues of courses "about" things do not compare; they only suggest a cushion of history or exposition between the student and some "subject," a cushion which textbooks neatly cut and stuff, and which the teacher adjusts to every learner's comfort. The curriculum of St.

John's College is not trimmed, padded, labeled, or adjustable. It makes inexorable demands which are the same for all. Nor are they impossible demands; they are indeed more practicable than any others, because more rewarding. It is assumed by those who avoid great books that such books are especially difficult. The contrary is true. Most of them were written for everybody, in "a basic language about everything." A classic is always fresh, vernacular, sensible, and responsible. Even the mathematical and scientific classics were written in a tradition which made them intelligible; if we have lost contact with that tradition, the thing to do is to regain it—by mastering its classics—so that we may cease to be the gapers at abstraction which half of us now are.

If the list is imperfect, it can be improved by those who have the learning and the will to do so. Its present relevance to liberal education is immense in any case, for it represents the first serious effort in contemporary America to build a single and rational curriculum suited to the needs of minds which have work to do, and which someday should be unwilling to forgive any system of education that had required of them less discipline than this. Education is honored when it is hard, but it is most honored when it is hard and good. The human mind naturally delights in exercise. Any student is to be envied who has passed this much through his mind, and any teacher who does so annually.

The great books of the West are in several languages, and the flawless situation would be one in which the student read them as Greek, Latin, Italian, Spanish, French, German, or Russian originals. Such a situation will never be; translations are necessary. But the necessity is not lamentable. The better a book the more meaning it keeps in translation; its value was not in its phrases. Style is wonderful, but sense and wisdom are more so. And it is no accident that many a modern literature has flourished most vigorously in those periods when translation flourished, pouring new floods of ideas into the contemporary pool.

The classics are so necessary to us that we resist them even while we accept them, as we do our parents. There is a perpetual battle of the books whose line sways forward or backward as the ancients or the moderns seem to be winning. The classics are alternately returned to and escaped from; men cannot live without them, but sometimes this means that they think they cannot live with them. The strange fact is that they are living with them even in the moment of victory over their great power. The power needed for victory had come from them. Both the yes and the no are answers to questions the classics have asked. It is a healthy sign when the answers are vigorous; when, for instance, controversy can rage among educators over the composition of the perfect list for a curriculum. It is a sad sign when there is no such controversy because there is no general belief in lists of books—that is to say, in books. All good lists will be much alike, for there are no alternatives to Homer, Plato, Shakespeare, Newton, and Tolstoy. But any time must be sure that its own list is right at the edges; and a time which does not care about this is simply not interested in itself, however much it thinks it is interested in current institutions and events.

The contemporary scene is filled with educators who want to protect students from the classics; which they do not burn but which they would keep on the back shelves. Their compassion, almost tearful at moments, is for a generation of youth threatened with direct exposure to the best spirits that have lived. Such an exposure, they say, imperils health and sanity in the tender and growing mind. Those educators should be asked whether they have read these books. The danger from them is the danger to plants from sun, rain, and enough wind to toughen their stems. The best books are none too good for the young.

The right reading of such books is never a passive affair. They require to be met on their own ground, which is the ground common to all good thought and imagination. That is why subsidiary disciplines—in language, in mathematics, in the art of discussion, and in the various arts of the laboratory—have to be planned. But this is what gives meaning to discipline, and makes it exciting. Colleges will differ with respect to the rings of studies they build about the central one. In so far as they are serious, they will agree to keep the center in plain view.

The great tradition is a tradition of change and growth; ideas have never stood still. It is also—and indeed for this very reason—astonishingly stable. Where there is so much life there is bound to be sturdiness; strength is not inconsistent with equilibrium. The principle is clear in mathematics no less than in literature. But it will not be clear to a student whose struggles with modern mathematics are struggles in a void where Euclid is silent, and where perspective upon Descartes is unobtainable. The story is one of revolutions, yet it is a story, and the mind of the student can master it in terms of permanence and progression. So can the mind of the student master the epic, always being written, of human virtue. The heroes of the epic—justice, hope, mercy, and courage—are perennially in danger from the intellect that ignores them or dismisses them as sleeping words.

The great writer wakes up the great words. It is he who lets us know that wise, noble, brave, honorable, temperate, and true are still the great adjectives, indestructible in their potency, and most exact. And it is he who gives us persons. Great literature is populated with persons, not to know whom is to be imperfectly alive. To be ignorant of the classics is to be ignorant of Achilles, Nestor, Agamemnon, Odysseus, Clytemnestra, Helen, Croesus, Solon, Alcibiades, Socrates, Electra, Orestes, Abraham, Moses, Samson, Solomon, David, Jesus, Monnica, Roland, Tristram, Lancelot, Beatrice, Farinata, Gargantua, Pantagruel, Panurge, Falstaff, Hamlet, Lear and his daughters, Rosalind, Prospero, Don Quixote, Sancho Panza, Gulliver, Robinson Crusoe, Squire Western, Sganarelle, Harpagon, Tartuffe, Alceste, D'Artagnan, Pangloss, Elizabeth Bennett, Rob Roy, Mr. Pickwick, Pendennis, Raskalnikov, Pierre Bezukhov, Prince Andrey, the Brothers Karamazov, Huckleberry Finn, Captain Ahab, Hester Prynne—the list seems endless, though it is not, since any aristocracy is limited in its size. These persons, like the books that contain them, are "a natural and irresistible aristocracy," says Thoreau, with "no cause of their own to plead." They want to convince us of nothing except themselves, and this they do. Not to know them argues oneself unknown.

The great books are the source from which wit and humor come, and all that is rangy in the mind. They are the headwaters of sense, and the reference when we are wise. Their authority is not the kind that makes us servile, for it is something we are proud to acknowledge; we lose nothing when we praise a fine day. We cannot copy them, for their authors were not copyists. "The great achievements of the past," says Whitehead, "were the adventures of the past."

That is why Thoreau can call them "the only oracles which are not decayed." There is no substitute for their nobility, their brightness, and their sanity. Nothing is equivalent to the Bible, there is no book like Aristotle's *Ethics,* no Platonist has ever remotely resembled the Plato who enchants and rebuilds us. Shakespeare is a universe, and Dante is another one. The great books are all different, yet their humanity makes them one. A golden thread connects their essential knowledge; Socrates demonstrates that justice is not what we do but are, and two thousand years later Hamlet remarks that to use every man after his desert is to use him after your own honor and dignity.

The great books are not useful in the world until they are widely known. They should be read early and late, and read everywhere. The writer who cannot depend upon their presence in the minds of many readers will have to be as poor as his readers; they support him as he communicates. They are the only source of future classics, for they are the one intellectual family that is fertile. A classic may appear at any time; they have not all been written yet; but this cannot happen without forebears, and it is a nice question how a generation unconscious of the classics would recognize a new one. The educated person knows a good book when he sees one, because he has seen good books before, and he is warned against even the best imitations. New classics do not imitate the old, except as truth imitates itself. The accent is always fresh, the tone is ever contemporary.

As teachers the great books are not competitors with life. "Anyone who can learn from life can learn from books," says Everett Dean Martin. It is obvious that many learn from neither, but that is because they are looking for truth as if it were in containers. Neither experience nor books

[157]

can be said to contain what is good for us in the way that bags hold beans. "Every author," says Pascal, "has a meaning in which all the contradictory passages agree, or he has no meaning at all." What a writer means at last is what experience tends to mean yet never states, just as he, being human, cannot do better than confess his humanity. "We expected to see an author, and we find a man." In great books we find man as he is when he is most free, sincere, and humble before truth in its ineffable variety.

To read the great books is to banish some of the chaos which ignorance of ourselves creates. This is because they are a mirror, but it is also because they are a company of minds. They draw us in, and their manners improve ours. Not the least virtue of a great book is that it is active all of the time; it works and plays tirelessly, so that our attention, following its progress, is steadily on the stretch. Its density is beyond the ordinary. It is easier to read than the relaxed and vacuous book, because it is more continuously worth while. Many men have found it so. That is why it is a classic.

Reading is a high art because it is a generous art, like listening. It is to writing as listening is to speaking, and the educated person does all four things more or less equally well. The good listener is universally loved, not alone because he flatters us but because in his presence the effort of speech justifies itself. We tire of those who cannot or will not understand us. Charity is required in the listener, and a willingness to receive whatever shall be given. So in the reader, who has learned how to surrender himself to his book. The good reader is not critical while he reads. To stop reading is criticism, but if the book continues to deserve attention it deserves the whole attention and the benefit of every doubt. The art of reading is among other things the art of adopting the pace the author has set. Some books are fast and some are slow, but no book can be understood if it is taken at the wrong speed. Criticism, when the time for it has come, is an act of imagination no less than of intellect. The good reader is not a prig, snooping for faults and errors. Neither is he cantankerous, or a sophist whose cleverness dissolves every idea before it has taken shape. He is the sensible man reading, the man who cannot be fooled forever, the man who wants the truth so much that he will heed every claim to it that he hears, but who when the claim is discovered to be false can be more contemptuous than any man. Reading is itself a kind of composition, as listening can seem to have its own eloquence. The four arts are forms of the same thing, discourse. The great writer had faith in his audience, and the great reader does not fail him even after centuries have passed.

The last person to go to for a definition of literature is the half-educated scientist, just as the last person who can speak for or against science is the literary man who knows nothing about it. The typical half-educated scientist might be Herbert Spencer, who puts literature among the "miscellaneous activities which make up the leisure part of life, devoted to the gratification of the tastes and feelings." The condescension in those words is as revolting as their ignorance is awful. "We yield to none," says Spencer, "in the value we attach to aesthetic culture and its pleasures." Such a man can know nothing of literature, which is no more for leisure than botany is. If it is not necessary it is nothing. Even Huxley, who was no barbarian, could say it was a source of "refined pleasure." Literature is coarse compared with physics, and for refinement it cannot touch mathematics. It is moral, and therefore practical. Its subject matter is the mad variety of men, and its conclusion is that nothing can be done about this except to suggest that as long as men are recognizable they must be of one kind. But the kind is radical and rough, a piece of nature which grace never wholly reforms. Literature is to the race, says Newman, what autobiography is to the individual; it is the "Life and Remains of the natural man."

Literature is more than style, form, and sensibility. It is the image of man as he moves. Elsewhere we get propositions about him or measurements of him, but here he is, half dust and half idea. The creators of literature become self-conscious from time to time and indulge in generalization concerning the species—the most pitiful of creatures, says Zeus in the *Iliad,* the most pernicious race of little odious vermin, says the King of Brobdingnag to Gulliver, the noblest work of God, says Pope—but their proper business is with his image, which can range all the way from conventional knights and clowns to the immortal individuals of Shakespeare. Not that the image is external merely, or irrelevant to us. The poet who paints the passions well, says Pascal, "has not shown us his own riches, but ours." Great literature is about its reader, the man who is always different and who never changes.

Great literature is story, which according to an ancient authority is not the same thing as history. But a good education in the one implies a good education in the other. Those whose sense of history is stiff or feeble will not be good readers of poetry, whose principal business is with story. Modern fiction confuses fiction with history; large portions of the public read novels only in order to learn about people or types of people they will never meet, in a foreign country, in a strange trade, on an unfamiliar economic level, or in another class. Novelists are expected to report life as it is being lived somewhere else, and it is assumed that other sorts of evidence would corroborate theirs. Another view of fiction, the traditional one, asks its authors to deal with the life all men live, and in doing so to render it both familiar and strange, since life is regularly the one as well as the other, a miracle no less than a monotony. Neither scholarship nor criticism keeps such a view alive today, with the result that fiction divides its strength between the pure fact of the social document and the pure fancy of the detective story. So in the case of history there are too few scholars who remind us as Jacques Barzun does that the power to diagnose the past "means seeing the familiar with the strange without losing the sense of either. History is not all strangeness nor all familiarity. It is as novel and as commonplace as life, which it recaptures."

History and story both recapture life, and they agree with each other in that they possess a wild theme, capable only of art's control. The man who is incompetent in literature will not bring to the reading of history the kind of knowledge that can make it live. It has been said that if the present generation had believed history, war would not have recurred. This can scarcely be true, but the capacity to believe history is the capacity to see many potentialities in men, and to understand that extremes of behavior are confined by no providence to the past. They remain possible, as literature could have told us if we had believed it too. The subject of literature is human possibility, which is not infinite but which is greater than complacency admits. The problem of history in the college is perplexing. No student can learn all of it, as for that matter no historian does. The best thing he can do is to study the great histories of Herodotus, Thucydides, Tacitus, Gibbon, and the rest; and to practice with their aid the art of diagnosis.

To know how to believe poetry and history is to know how to feel. It is also to know how to think, but when these two things are done deeply they are forms of the same life. We do not trust a brain without a heart, and we cannot respect a heart without a brain. It is often said, and with justice, that the contemporary world is badly educated in its feelings. The simplest evidence is the behavior of audiences at movies which are trying to be tragedies. In proportion as the attempt is successful the audiences are embarrassed, for nothing has trained them in the emotions of pity and terror; they are afraid to be afraid, and they do not know whom to pity, or when; pity is confused with sympathy, while fear is felt as a weakness. The embarrassment expresses itself in titters or in audible signs of disgust; they came to be moved a little, but not this much. They brought quantities of sentiment which they cannot use, for the work of art before them is aiming at precision, and understanding is required. The sentimental man is falsely intellectual; he feels situations, not persons, he lets himself be moved only when convention tells him it is right to do so. Tragedy is for those who can feel the predicaments of persons, and who will do so even if the situations of these persons have not existed before. Tragedy is always new; it tests our power to respond when nothing will have prepared a response except our education in the length, breadth, depth of life. To experience tragedy is not to be disturbed but to be further settled in understanding. Tragedy itself is education.

But we do not pay it the honor of saying so, just as in

most of our discussions concerning lyric poetry we miss the point of its connection with emotion. We ask the poet to show us how much he feels, since we still cherish a vague notion that feeling is important, but we do not demand of him the clear tone that sounds when feeling has been accepted, measured, and inclosed. Not destroyed, for only sentiment can do that. But placed in the strange perspective where it belongs, and where clarity concerning it is the best proof that its power is known. We are the victims of our fear lest we feel all the way to a conclusion. The popular conspiracy to ignore death, which expresses itself in so many circumlocutions for the words "he died," is the most familiar example of our stopping short of the terrible fact. To fear death in the beginning is to fear it less in the end. But we obscure the end, and so accumulate in ourselves a charge of feeling which has no work to do. It is not that we do not feel enough. It is rather that our feeling seldom fits the situation. That is why we seem to feel less than we do, and why we learn so little from the experience.

The greatly sensitive person is intelligent concerning the limits of reason but he desires to reach them. The man who knows how to feel is the last man to despise thought. "Peace is the understanding of tragedy, and at the same time its preservation." For without tragedy man loses his dignity, which is the dignity, says Pascal, "of a deposed king." He does not know, for instance, how to distinguish between failures. Some failures are contemptible, but some are heroic. The tendency at present is to dismiss them all as pieces of bad luck. The failure of a tragic hero elevates him in our eyes; he has taught us by exploring the realms of decision. He knew how to make decisions in darkness; he could face facts both as intelligible and as unintelligible

[163]

things, and now we can measure the space between those poles. The world is as intelligible as we make it, and the failures of great men, no less than their successes, are a part of our education in possibility. It is no coincidence that when the art of tragedy has flourished it has risen out of religious ritual; for the essence of drama is the conflict between darkness and light, the unknown and the known. The tragic hero is one who has died dissecting the unknown.

The art of tragedy is a fine art, as lyric poetry is on its lesser scale. Both use words, but their forms are no more literal than the forms of music, painting, and sculpture. The fine artist in any of his aspects is an educator whom the student must accept, but his message is not verbal. He should be encountered in his own tongue, with the least possible intervention by other teachers. A minimum of intervention is necessary, as in the case of the great books; it should confine itself, however, to the assurance that the student remembers what he hears and sees, and that he understands it to the limit of his ability.

The fine artist is doing one of the most difficult things a man can do. He is rendering an account of life in terms of its irreducible particulars. He may not put it this way himself, and he probably should not. His attention is all upon the particular—the man Hamlet, the phrase Mozart will glorify into a symphony—with which he has fallen in love. It is apparently meaningless, but its effect upon us is not the effect of innumerable other individual things which we regard and pass. It tells us about everything else in the world at the same time that it tells us about itself. It not only exists, it symbolizes existence. The artist was right in saying it was nothing but an object he had loved, and we as critics will be right in letting the statement stand, even for ourselves, who cannot claim to be authorities on existence either. Nevertheless, it is true that a part has expressed the whole, an accident has achieved essence; and the student, in addition to the things he does with style, tone, line, rhythm, accent, and material, should be encouraged to contemplate this miracle. It is a miracle that happens once in a while outside of art—when, for instance, the chance sight of a face or a landscape organizes the world. The fine artist aims to control the occurrence so that he may repeat it at will. His infrequent success is reflected in our judgment that most works of art are not inspired. That is as good a way of putting it as any.

The student who does not "appreciate" fine art will learn none of its meaning from the vicarious raptures of a teacher. The rapture is his own business, which is better done when the rest of his education has been good; when he has mastered language to the point where this new language of art can more or less readily reveal its structure; when he himself is an artist in the one and the many, the like and the unlike, the strange and the familiar, the better and the worse. If his imagination is not free already, and accustomed to exercise, it will make little headway now, nor has the teacher of "appreciation" any right to complain when the result is resistance rather than rapture. The fine arts are not extras. They have their necessity too, and it is as practical as wisdom or joy. But the student whose education has been good will scarcely need to be told this. Fine art is not religion, and it is more than a plaything for those who have no other use for their hands. The good student will know what it is.

VOCATION

Liberal education is sometimes distinguished from useful education, but the foregoing pages should have made it clear that the distinction is unfortunate and false. All education is useful, and none is more so than the kind that makes men free to possess their nature. Knowledge and skill to such an end are ends in themselves, past which there is no place for the person to go. It is both useful and liberal to be human, just as it takes both skill and knowledge to be wise. If education is not practical when it teaches men to do the things which become men, then no education is practical.

The distinction, however, has something else in mind. Any man does particular things, and the question arises whether his education should not be directed to those things alone, first as well as last. There is a thing called vocational education, and the emphasis upon its virtues is great in our time. It is not universally admitted that humanity is a vocation of sufficient importance to justify the expense of colleges devoted solely to its study. So technical studies are preferred.

The distinction is still false. Technique was the Greek word for art, and there is a human art which dominates all other arts, since it is the art that teaches them. It teaches them how men do what they do. To miss this lesson is not to know what human work is. It is not even to be prepared for a profession. But the professions are less intellectual than they once were, and so they make a diminishing demand for prepared persons. They are satisfied with preparatory studies, which are quite a different thing. The

[166]

result is that they can count on even less competence than used to be the case. This is because our liberal education is bad; it is not technical enough in its own way; it misses intellectual precision. But one of the reasons it is bad is that the professions do not insist upon its being good. They will do so as soon as they give up trying to be trades. Even the advanced study of literature is a trade. Many who pride themselves upon being liberal because they pursue this trade are as ignorant of most other things as any mechanical engineer could be of metaphysics. They call their periodicals, humorously, trade journals. That is what they are, and they are useless to any world for which literature is made.

No antipathy appears between technical and liberal education if we remember that both are concerned with art. It has already been said that liberal education suffers today from its ignorance of the liberal arts. But technical education suffers also because it does not know the meaning of its name; because it is willing to accept students whose training has not been general enough to make them recognize principles when they appear; because it identifies the useful with the utilitarian, and so blunts that very sense of the concrete which it requires. For not to see the truth in a thing is not to see the thing. If liberal education is concerned with truth, and technical education with things, then the two could teach each other. The first needs to be more conscious of its operations, and the second needs to be more theoretical than it is. Liberal education, that is to say, should discover in what ways it can be technical—how it can teach the arts of reading, writing, measuring, remembering, and imagining—and technical education should acknowledge that it also is intellectual. It is true that graduate and professional schools are beginning to ask that the students who come to them from college be more liberally prepared. But the colleges do not know at the moment what this means. Having survived the chaos of the elective system by transforming themselves into preprofessional institutions, and having found that in a way this worked, they are puzzled when they hear that the great schools above them are not satisfied with the way. They know they should teach something, but they still have to know that it is the liberal arts. The medical schools are aware of this if no other institutions are. It may be that the reform of the college will come from the professions after all: from their discovery that what they need most is good minds to work with, and that the first thing a doctor, lawyer, priest, or engineer has to be is a person.

The most painful single thing about contemporary American education is the system of "vocational choice" which extends down as far as the high schools. In college this would be an evil, and in fact it is; but even the high school student is nagged until he declares what he wants to do when he grows up. The boy who knows that much about himself is one out of a thousand. The rest pretend they know; and from that moment are channeled toward a life which they may not discover to be the wrong one until they are middle-aged. All men are specialists at last, but there is a time for choice and it is not the time of youth. Youth wants to be all things at once, and should be given a go at it. When the experiment is done, a specialty will announce itself. Meanwhile there is not the hurry we suppose there is—and so supposing, threaten our society with a caste system of predestined trades and professions such as democracy may find it difficult to survive.

VII

The Arts of Teaching and Being Taught

THE LIBERAL arts have been said by Mortimer Adler to be "nothing but the arts of teaching and being taught." If teaching and studying are imagined on their highest level, and if it is understood that great books as well as men may qualify as teachers, the definition is not oversimplified. The great books are necessary. So, however, are the men; and it is always important that men should think it honorable to be teachers. When the profession is apologetic, society is not sound. "Whom the gods hate they make schoolmasters," said Lucian. But that is true only if the gods hate men. For the gods know, even if we do not, that man is in a special sense the teachable animal. When dogs and monkeys are taught, the aim is to make them resemble another species, usually man. But men must be taught to resemble themselves. Only by education can they be said to become the kind of animal they are.

The responsibility of the teacher is so great that a full vision of it can be crushing. He has persons in his charge. The fact should sober him; but he hears in addition that he is responsible for the entire society which these persons represent. The size of the assignment suggests that only madmen would dare to accept it, and that such is the meaning of Lucian's sentence. But it is not as serious as all that. The teacher needs only to remember that he is neither deity nor engine; he is a man, and in proportion as he succeeds at his calling he will be surrounded by more men. He and they are society.

The liberal education that has been described in the foregoing pages, and not only described but recommended for all, needs more good teachers than now exist. The requisite number must exist, even if it takes a thousand years to produce them—that is, to educate them. They will need to have better habits than most teachers today even pretend to have. But that will never be unless some teachers in our time consent to change their own habits; the race to come must have its ancestors.

The first habit to be changed is that of assuming that all one needs to know is one's own subject. In any college a given teacher will be biased toward some form of knowledge that agrees with his nature; indeed, unless he loves particular truths he cannot make his students love truth at all. But in a good college he will unite this love with a sense of what every student is there for: the common understanding which men need. He will try to know his colleagues as well as himself; and he will believe as they do in the single, central task of the institution. This is to produce a world whose citizens know the same things, and the indispensable things; and this without the regimentation which the anarchy of our present system threatens.

Good teachers have always been and will always be, and there are good teachers now. The necessity henceforth is that fewer of them be accidents. The area of accident is reduced when there is a design which includes the education of teachers. Not the training—a contemporary term that suggests lubricating oil and precision parts, not to say reflexes and responses. The design is less for institutions that turn out teachers than for a whole view of education that sees them as being naturally made when they teach themselves, with the help of one another and their students.

"It makes no difference to me," said Comenius, "whether I teach or am taught." If Socrates was the perfect teacher, the reason is that he was the perfect student. His suspicion of the Sophists was based upon the fact that their primary desire was not to learn. They preferred to lecture, and their capital was catchwords which they used over and over again, with no warning to the listener that the meanings had shifted. The teacher learns by teaching, which is the highest form of study. The more wisdom he shares, the more he keeps; for wisdom is shared when we ask real questions, and when we want answers no matter what the source, be it ourselves or others, be it old or young, be it one in authority or the most insignificant subordinate.

Such a teacher creates in a sense his own school. "Happy the natural college," says Emerson, "thus self-instituted around every natural teacher." There is no substitute for the natural teacher, and no formula whereby he may be made. But his kind is more numerous in certain situations than in others, and the best hope for education is a landscape of learning in which he will belong. When men seriously want to be educated, says Newman, "when they aim at something precise, something refined, something really luminous, something really large, something choice, they avail themselves, in some shape or other, of the ancient method of oral instruction, of present communication between man and man, of teachers instead of teaching, of the personal influence of a master, and the humble initiation of a disciple. . . . If we wish to become exact and fully furnished in any subject of teaching which is diversified and complicated, we must consult the living man and listen to his living voice. . . . The general principles of any study you may learn by books at home; but the detail, the color, the tone, the air, the life which makes it live in us, you must catch all these from those in whom it lives already."

This is the right doctrine, despite the fact that indolent and eccentric men have taken advantage of it. Unique individual charm is not the final virtue of a teacher. The charm should be personal, meaning that the thought behind it should be better than other thought, not merely different. The most personal thing about Socrates was not his nose or his voice but his love of wisdom. "He who thinks," the friend of Phaedrus said under the plane tree, "that only in principles of justice and goodness and nobility taught and communicated orally for the sake of instruction and graven in the soul is there clearness and perfection and seriousness —this is the right sort of man." The desire of the true teacher is not to triumph but to teach, and in teaching to learn. The teacher without charm is negligible, but the teacher without anything else is contemptible; and he is most contemptible when he courts applause. The good college is the natural college in so far as it is a place where the personal wisdom of older men, grounded deeply enough in the great tradition to be free wisdom, modifies younger men. But the art of education can assist nature here, as art always assists nature, by providing more opportunity than exists for colleges to be what they can.

The good teacher is a man whose conversation is never

finished, partly because it is about real things and so cannot be finished, but partly because there is always a new audience, which itself takes part. The student in learning teaches himself and his teacher. How he learns remains something of a mystery, for there is an artist in him, the teachable man, who has his own devices and proceeds to his own conclusions. The art of being taught is the art of letting the nature of learning take its course. It is a course which the teacher can free from many obstacles, and to which he can give formal aid; but he does not invent it any more than the student does. The student does not decide to have the mind with which he educates himself. He uses the one he has, both for the things that can be taught him and for those he must possess through his own effort, or according to his own desire; for just as the good teacher loves some particular knowledge more than any other, so the good student will range beyond the prescriptions of the curriculum, reading what his genius pleases in addition to what his nature requires.

The teacher will encourage these excursions. "Who is so stupidly curious as to send his son to school in order that he may learn what the teacher thinks?" This question of St. Augustine's will be remembered by a good teacher whenever he is tempted to suppress some novelty in a student's thought. It may or may not lead to knowledge, but if it is the student's own discovery it has a present importance which had better not be doubted. There is a skill in instruction, but St. Thomas Aquinas has pointed out that there is also a skill in discovery, and it is our own discoveries that best persuade us. The art of being taught is the art of discovery, as the art of teaching is the art of assisting discovery to take place.

[173]

Discovery can take place only if the relation between the teacher and the student is one of mutual respect. It is especially important that the teacher should respect the student, and it will be easy for him to do so if he assumes that the student is someone from whom he may learn. Then it will be the discovery that is mutual, though courtesy in the teacher will exaggerate this. The teacher is courteous because he is respectful, and because that is the way in which courtesy is taught. But his respect is for the subject too, which means that although he loves the student he is sometimes obligated to be severe. The teacher is kind, but to someone he is training to forget him. "My son is coming to do without me," wrote Emerson in his Journal. "And I am coming to do without Plato." The good teacher disappears out of the student's life as Virgil and Beatrice disappear out of *The Divine Comedy.* They are remembered as persons, and so is every good teacher remembered; but when the student has found his own way in the world he cannot recall how much of his wisdom he owes to another. It is his now, and that is what his teacher had intended.

The teacher who desires evidence that his students are interested should also ask for evidence that they are disinterested—that they understand what he is saying. For if they understand him they are sharing with him the experience of thought, which is not an individual experience. The true teacher is singularly innocent of ambition to be praised, loved, or remembered. He is, in fact, the best secular image of the innocent man. And the student respects no other man, least of all one who is crafty or worldly. He will see plenty of worldly men in his time, and their craft will surpass that of any mistaken teacher. It is only in the long run that the innocent man turns out to have been right. The last things learned will agree with him, and then perhaps he will be remembered. But across the "labyrinth of the world," as Comenius puts it, the student and the teacher will share in silence that "paradise of the heart" where agreement is more than a matter of debit and credit.

The teacher, of course, must have authority over the student before he can be respected in the way the student wants to respect him. But authority comes naturally with knowledge that is lucid as the liberal arts make knowledge lucid. The teacher who is not a liberal artist may indoctrinate or charm, but he will not teach. Indoctrination makes the teacher's thought prevail, but teaching is less a matter of what either the teacher or the student thinks than of what the mind itself, the third person, decides and says. The teacher will conceal none of his authority, for he is democrat enough to know that its purpose is to strengthen the student against the time when he will have to choose between accepting and rejecting it. Authority exists only to be denied by better authority; its best act is to destroy itself. The teacher is successful at the moment when his student becomes original. He must be "a kind of fate to his pupil," says Lane Cooper, "and at the same time must bestow upon him the supreme good gift of free will. . . . The original sin of the individual must be scourged and purged away; his original goodness must be cherished and encouraged." If this imputes a kind of divinity to the teacher, that is precisely what some students do. They are wrong, and every teacher knows it; but the good teacher is able to interpret and forgive the blasphemy, meanwhile letting the shadow it casts upon him measure the depth of his duty.

The education of teachers is an education in the liberal arts. When this education is good, and falls on the right ground, it produces persons with usable intellects and imaginations who know both what and why they are teaching. A teacher who can answer neither of those questions is no teacher, for thus he proves himself incapable of the one pleasure reserved for him among the pleasures possible to man: the pleasure of being intelligible. Human communication, so difficult and so rare, is his professed assignment, and at the moment in his students' lives when such success as is achieved will count forever. It will count in their understanding, and so in their happiness. It will also count, by making them more communicative themselves, in the happiness of mankind.

One kind of contemporary teacher lacks the courage of his authority, which he misconceives as authority is commonly misconceived. He thinks it is power. But power has no authority in the region of intellect and morals. Authority there is excellence in knowledge and art; and excellence in such things has indeed a special power which only the initiated know. The special power of the teacher is revealed in the competence of his search for the fundamental questions to be asked—questions fundamental enough to engage all men, so that argument can be reventilated and revived.

The search for such questions, when it does go on today, is often mistaken for its opposite. The search is itself an argument, but it is accused of a desire to stop argument forever. Curiosity about initial questions is confused with propaganda for final answers. The tolerance we practice in matters of opinion is the tolerance not of hope but of despair, as a recent distinction has it. We do not trust argument unless it is aimless—without, in other words, the background of an agreement that the purpose of it is the discovery of truth. We do not trust truth, which we identify only with those who have told lies in its name. Truth is remote, but not to care how remote it is puts one in Dante's dark circle of those who lived without blame and without praise, but were for themselves; who from cowardice made the great refusal; who lost the good of the intellect, and so were never alive.

"To be indifferent which of two opinions is true," says John Locke in language very different from Dante's, "is the right temper of the mind that preserves it from being imposed on, and disposes it to examine with that indifferency till it has done its best to find the truth. But to be indifferent whether we embrace falsehood or truth is the great road to error." All opinions are to be tolerated for what they are worth, but the person today who endeavors to compare opinions by applying a scale of worth is seldom tolerated. His scale may be wrong, but that is not why he is criticized. There is no common search for a right scale that would make such criticism possible. The open mind is one which has begun to think, but we act as if it were one which had stopped doing so because thought can be serious and dangerous, and because it is hard work. We do not doubt well. The good doubter doubts something; we dismiss everything. One sign of this is that we think it beneath our dignity to agree—the typical professor takes no position, either his own or any other's. He calls this tolerance, and does not seem to mind that it is tolerance of bad thinking as well as good. The thing not to be tolerated is bad thinking. Perhaps Locke has explained why there is so much of it today. Cynicism paralyzes argument.

The last generation of students may never forgive its teachers who taught contempt and fear of truth. The distinction they made was the one between fact and opinion, not the one between opinion and truth. The difference itself is a fact, to be ignorant of which is neither to be armed against opinion nor to have one's own. The immediate danger is that we shall have a riot of ill-considered slogans. "Respect for the truth is an acquired taste," and the recovery of it may take a long time, for it involves an understanding that freedom has its own compulsions, and it requires a discipline in the adjustment of thought to thought which only the liberal arts can teach. To say that truth is better than falsehood is not to speak vaguely. It is more powerful, it is more interesting, and it is less lonely. "There is but one world in common for those who are awake," said Heraclitus, "but when men are asleep each turns away into a world of his own." It is the love of truth that makes men free in the common light of day.

Index

INDEX

INDEX

INDEX